WHAT THE HECK IS A GRAPE NUT?

Edited by Ty Reynolds

Script:
the writers' group

Calgary, Alberta, Canada

Published by Script: the writers' group inc.

Copyright © 1991 by the Canadian Broadcasting Corporation and Script: the writers' group inc.

Cover design by Ty Reynolds

Individual questions and answers in this book were first broadcast by CBC Radio stations across Canada and are used with permission. The CBC logo is also used with permission.

Manufactured in Canada

10 9 8 7 6 5 4 3 2 1 91 92 93 94 95 96 97 98 99

Canadian Cataloguing in Publication Data

Main entry under title:

What the heck is a grape nut?

ISBN 0-9694287-6-6

1. Questions and answers.   I. Reynolds, Ty, 1956-

AG195.W43 1991   031.02   C91-090632-7

Printed in Canada

Where did these questions and answers come from?

The questions in this book were spawned in the enquiring minds of CBC listeners from coast to coast. Radio shows that contributed questions are

Daybreak (Kelowna)
The Eyeopener (Calgary)
Edmonton AM (Edmonton)
The Morning Edition (Regina)
Morning North (Sudbury)
CBO Morning (Ottawa)
Information Morning (Fredericton)
Information Morning (Saint John)
Island Morning (Charlottetown)
Information Morning (Halifax)

The answers to the questions in this book represent the research of many people who work for CBC Radio across Canada. CBC staff were helped out by hundreds of individuals and organizations who provided the information and expertise necessary to answer these Good Questions. To both these groups of people, we offer our appreciation.

Particular thanks are extended to regular information supply lines at federal, provincial, and municipal government departments and agencies.

Who made this book possible?

A portion of the purchase price of this book is being donated to local charities. The donation of proceeds to charity is only possible due to the contributions of time, supplies, and services by the businesses involved in the production and distribution of this book. We would like to thank

Coles Bookstores Ltd. and all the independent booksellers who participated by carrying this book,

Canadian Air Cargo, Canadian Airlines International,

Script: the writers' group inc.,

Greyhound Courier Express,

Acadian Bus Lines,

and

United Graphics (1991)

for their kindness and generosity.

Introduction

Hi! I'm Arthur Black, but you can think of me as the doorman, about to introduce you to an all-you-can-eat smorgasbord festively entitled *What the Heck is a Grape Nut?*

Before we start grazing, I've got a confession to make.

I'm a thief.

It comes with the territory. In a typical week, I write three or four radio commentaries, a syndicated newspaper column, plus perhaps a couple of speeches, a magazine article, and—who knows?—maybe even a book preface.

I need, then, about ten new ideas a week. Five hundred and twenty a year.

There are two or three ways for an average Canuck to pull that off. He can arrange for a brain exchange with Robertson Davies. He can ingest Ben Johnsonian quantities of psychotropic drugs ...

Or he can be a thief.

I steal ideas everywhere and anywhere I can. I eavesdrop in elevators and taverns. I make mental notes in cafeteria lineups and airport departure lounges.

Then of course, there's the printed word. I lift ideas from newspapers and magazines—not to mention matchbook covers and highway billboards.

But it's a typing-finger-to-mouth existence, never knowing where your next bit of inspirational booty will come from. That's why I was delighted to lay my Fagin clutches on a copy of *That's A Good Question!* two years ago. Imagine! A hundred thought-provoking posers thought up by CBC listeners—the very folks I spend most of my time talking to!

I wasted no time sitting down to read. And steal.

Since then, we've had son of *That's A Good Question!*—called *That's A Good Question, Canada!*

And now this pithy piece of provocation entitled *What the Heck is a Grape Nut?*

I don't know, but I intend to find out.

Oh, and if you should happen to hear something about Grape Nut origins on *Basic Black* next Saturday, well ... just between you and me, eh?

ARTHUR BLACK
HOST, *BASIC BLACK*

NOVEMBER, 1991

Table of Contents

Why do smoke alarms have radioactive material in them?

Smoke alarms contain a small amount of amarithium 241, which is an isotope of uranium. The amarithium 241 causes the air around it to ionize, producing electricity. If smoke enters the passage that contains the amarithium 241, the smoke is ionized and a voltage shift occurs. This change in current trips the alarm.

The level of radioactivity in the smoke alarm is regulated and monitored by the Underwriters Laboratory of Canada (ULC). The risk of exposure to radiation from a smoke alarm has been compared by the ULC to the risk of exposure to solar radiation when flying from Toronto to Vancouver. To put the hazard in some perspective, the ULC calculates that there could be limited risk to your health if you placed your head two and a half inches from a smoke alarm and left it there for a continuous one-year period.

When smoke alarms were introduced, it was required by law that they be disposed of by returning them to the manufacturer or to the Atomic Energy Control Board. Today, fire departments in some communities accept old smoke alarms for disposal as part of their hazardous waste programs. However, in most communities, they are simply tossed in the garbage.

Smoke detectors have a life span of about 20 years. They should be vacuumed about once a year to keep the sensor passage free of dust build-up.

Why do athletes wear black under their eyes?

Many professional sports are played under intense light, whether from the sun, television lights, or stadium lights during night games. This light can reflect off a player's cheeks, creating sufficient glare to impair his or her play.

Since black absorbs light, glare can be reduced by darkening the cheeks. Traditionally, the black smear was made with burnt cork and later with greasepaint, but many athletes today apply a bandage specifically manufactured for this purpose. The bandage is easily removed, and doesn't run like cheap mascara.

The strange make-up may not look pretty, but in the big leagues, "the sun was in my eyes" does not cut it as an excuse for a bungled play.

Since houseflies can't fly upside down, how do they land on the ceiling?

The housefly is not aerodynamically designed to fly upside down, yet it is able to land safely at any angle, even upside down. To do so at the high speeds at which flies fly, the fly must perform some acrobatics.

Before attaching itself to an overhead surface, the fly must fly rightside up very close to where it wants to land. Then the fly reaches up with its front legs to make contact with the surface. Once anchored, the fly swings its body over in a forward flip for a perfect six-point landing.

The front legs of the average housefly are about three millimetres long, with an average overhead reach of one and a half millimetres.

How does a lit candle reduce the smoke and smell of cigarettes in a room?

A few burning candles will go a long way toward clearing the air at your next house party. And it's a lot more friendly than greeting your guests from behind a gas mask.

Candles reduce smoke and odour because they produce charcoal, particles of carbon left over after the burning process. Charcoal is an effective filtering agent, used in such products as water filters.

Charcoal particles have long thin pores that can trap organic molecules that cause odours. When a charcoal particle meets a particle of tobacco smoke, the charcoal absorbs the tobacco smoke into its pores, eliminating it from the air. The charcoal particles, laden with smoke molecules and other impurities, then settle as dust.

How did Thousand Island salad dressing get its name?

Thousand Island dressing and its name date back to 1924. The name comes from the Thousand Islands in the St. Lawrence River, which are located where the river is fed by Lake Ontario. The dressing was the creation of an unnamed chef from the Waldorf Astoria Hotel in New York City. This chef, also credited with the creation of veal oscar, was invited to work his culinary magic at Boldt Castle on one of the Thousand Islands.

The new dressing was designed with the location in mind. Thousand Island dressing is based on Russian dressing with the addition of pickles, cream, green peppers, and seasonings. The bits and pieces of the ingredients are supposed to resemble a thousand islands in a river of dressing.

Why is there a crescent moon on outhouse doors?

The outhouse moon is one of those ubiquitous symbols that is immediately understood by anyone who has had occasion to use an outdoor privy.

The traditional outhouse symbol dates back to the American colonial period. Since many of the settlers travelling to their homesteads were illiterate or from non-English-speaking countries, hotels needed simple symbols so their guests could identify which was the appropriate water closet. A crescent moon was used to indicate the women's facilities, and a star was used for the men's.

The use of these symbols soon spread to private outhouses, where gender-specific seating arrangements were unnecessary. Eventually the moon, being the simpler of the two symbols, "eclipsed" the star and became the only loo locator needed.

Where does the hockey term "to deke" come from?

The slang term for a fake shot on goal is believed to have first appeared in print in a 1960 *Time* magazine article titled "The Deke Man." The article was about the talents of Dickie Moore, a left-winger for the Montreal Canadiens. Moore is a 12-year veteran of the Habs, including six Stanley Cup championship seasons.

According to *Time*, "On the ice, Moore is one of the league's best players in the split-second art of faking a goalie out of position. 'I've developed a little play of my own,' he said.' It's kind of a fake shot. We call them dekes, for decoys.'"

Moore said he developed the shot to beat Detroit goalie Harry Lumley, who had a fake move of his own. When Moore stickhandled his way down the ice to score on Lumley, the goalie would leave a corner of the net for Moore to shoot into. But at the the last second, Lumley would cover the open corner to beat Moore's shot. Moore's deke was to fake a shot to the open corner, then quickly shoot the puck to another part of the net. Lumley, who was going for the open corner, was then caught off guard, thereby creating another scoring opportunity for Moore.

According to the *Dictionary of Canadianisms*, both "deke" and "deek" are correct spellings.

Who are those people behind Peter Mansbridge on the *National*?

Television news, like any other TV programming, goes through changes of fashion. It used to be that local TV news programs were broadcast from a studio. Then it became the vogue to broadcast the news from the newsroom. With chattering typewriters and bustling journalists in the background, the news was thought to look more real and immediate and less packaged. The bright lights, cables, and cameras were found to be a hindrance to the efficient operation of the newsroom, however. Practical considerations eventually took precedence, and the anchor desk was moved back to the studio.

Network news broadcasts are different. The people behind the anchor desk on the CBC national news are not merely "news central" props. They are working on the program even as it is on the air.

The two people directly behind Mansbridge run the closed captions for the hearing impaired. They begin work early in the afternoon, but also work during the newscast, entering late scripts and last-minute changes into the computer.

The third person in the background is the line-up editor. This person decides on the relative importance of each story and the order in which they will run. Although the sequence of the news stories is determined before the program goes to air, there are often changes at the last minute, and even during the broadcast. The line-up editor is also responsible for handling any emergencies during the newscast.

There are usually several other people on the set when major news stories are happening, such as during wars or political upheavals. These are journalists specifically assigned to cover these stories. Because of the late-breaking nature of these stories, the journalists are kept close at hand.

WHO ARE THOSE PEOPLE BEHIND
PETER MANSBRIDGE ON THE NATIONAL?

What is the real story behind the Man on the Moon logo on Proctor & Gamble products?

For years, stories have been circulating about the Proctor & Gamble logo. These stories claim that the logo is satanic, or is proof that the company is under the control of the Reverend Sun Myung Moon and his Unification Church, even though Reverend Moon holds no shares in the company. The supposed religious or satanic significance of the Proctor & Gamble logo has even been discussed in such forums of international debate as Ann Landers' newspaper column.

The stories aren't true, and the company appears to have been the victim of a smear campaign. Proctor & Gamble has taken the matter seriously, setting up a special hotline in an attempt to locate the source of the rumours. In the ten years since the hotline was installed, Proctor & Gamble has responded to 150,000 calls. The company also filed several lawsuits in 1982.

The Proctor & Gamble logo evolved from a simple and practical symbol. Beginning in 1851, the company marked its crates with a cross in a circle. This was so that illiterate dock workers could identify the crates, which otherwise looked the same as every other crate in the shipyard. The cross was later modified into a star. In a fit of patriotism, the star was changed to 13 stars, a reference to the original 13 states. Later, William A. Proctor added the quarter moon. The complete design has been the Proctor & Gamble logo ever since.

What the heck is a grape nut?

Grape Nuts cereal is not made from grapes or nuts. And there is no such thing in nature as a grape nut. Grape Nuts is merely the product name given to a brand of breakfast cereal. Grape Nuts is a blend of whole wheat and barley toasted in such a way that it doesn't turn soggy in milk. This characteristic makes it a popular ingredient in such other products as muffins and ice cream.

Grape Nuts was created by Charles Post in 1897. Post was an associate with the Kellogg brothers of breakfast cereal fame, but he soon had a falling out with them. Post began his own company with a cereal-based beverage called Postum. Although the product has sold for many years, it was not enough to keep the company growing.

Post experimented with crumbled sheets of baked wheat and other cereals. He eventually settled on a mixture of whole wheat and malt barley. After the wheat and barley mixture was toasted, the sheets were shredded and toasted again. During the toasting process, the mixture produces a sugar called dextrose. At that time, dextrose was more commonly known as grape sugar. Post felt that his new breakfast cereal had a nutty flavour, so he called it Grape Nuts.

Post had a flair for marketing, and he exploited the popular notion that his product was especially healthy. In that era of snakeoil salesmen and outrageous medical claims, newspaper articles were written extolling the healthful attributes and curative powers of the new cereal. Among its other qualities, Grape Nuts cured appendicitis, tightened up loose teeth, and made one smarter. Post even produced a newsletter that brought the public up to date on all the latest claims. He enclosed a copy in every box.

What is the origin of the widow's walk?

The widow's walk, introduced in colonial times, is an observatory deck on the top of a house. It was originally designed for houses near the ocean. From this vantage point, women could anxiously watch for their husband's ships returning home from sea.

The design feature isn't found only on houses near the sea, however. The widow's walk was brought to the prairies in the 1880s and was common on farm houses built up until the First World War. The architectural element was one of several copied from the Queen and Revival dwellings of the Victorian period. The widow's walk continued to be useful to farm wives, even if there was much less chance of discovering that one had become a widow. At harvest time, women used the walk to check up on the menfolk before preparing meals. The walk was also used to locate cows in the field when it came time to round them up.

What is the significance of the the pin Bill Cosby wears on his TV show?

The small pin Bill Cosby wears on his top-rated television program has the letters SD on it. Cosby had the one-of-a-kind pin specially made in memory of Sammy Davis Jr. The singer-dancer-actor credited with opening many doors for black entertainers died of throat cancer on May 16, 1990.

Bill Cosby and Sammy Davis Jr. had been close friends for many years, although they had never worked together prior to a recent guest appearance by Davis on the Cosby program. Cosby wears the pin in his friend's memory.

Where do carrot seeds come from?

From seed packets at the gardening store, as any seed catalogue will tell you. Of course, a *true* gardener may want to get them the old-fashioned way—from carrots.

Carrots are biennials, which means they produce seeds in their second year. Most carrots don't get a chance to turn to seed, however, since they are harvested and sent to market in their first year.

It is not difficult to produce carrot seeds. Begin with a carrot crop. If a carrot crop is intended as food, then the carrot sprouts are thinned out to give the sprouts that remain enough room in which to grow large roots. But if the crop is grown to produce seeds, then this step is unnecessary. In fact, a seed farmer wants to grow as many sprouts as possible.

In cooler climates, seed carrots are harvested each fall. The carrot tops are then cut off and stored over the winter. In temperate zones, the carrots are left in the ground.

In spring, the carrot tops are planted again. The tops develop new roots and begin to flower. The carrot flower is palm-sized and creamy white. At the end of the growing season, the flowers produce seed, and the cycle starts all over again.

Why does a baseball pitcher stand on a mound?

The pitcher's mound became an official part of baseball diamond geography in 1903. Before that, pitchers were at field level on a spot in the middle of the diamond. Since the pitching area gets more wear and tear than any other part of the field—even more than home plate—the pitcher's space was constantly torn up. Rain turned that part of the field into a veritable bog.

The solution was the pitcher's mound. The elevation of the mound provided the necessary drainage to keep the centre of the field relatively mud-free. The mound was originally 18 feet in diameter and 15 inches at the summit. This proved to be too high, and batters were having trouble hitting balls pitched to them. The summit was lowered to 10 inches in 1969.

The pitcher's mound isn't just any old hill—it must conform to the official rules. The pitcher toes up to something called a rubber as he prepares his toss. The rubber marks the pitcher's space on the diamond, just as home plate defines the batter's position. For the toss to be legal, the pitcher must be in contact with the rubber as the ball is released. The rubber is located 18 inches behind the centre of the mound, and the distance from the front edge of the rubber to the back of home plate is 60 feet and six inches. The slope of the mound begins six inches from the front edge of the rubber and must slope for six feet. To each side of the pitcher, the slope starts 18 inches from the rubber. The slope begins 22 inches behind the rubber.

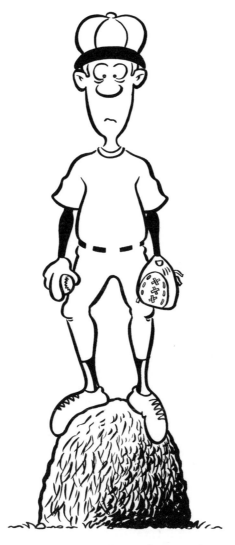

WHY DOES A BASEBALL PITCHER STAND ON A MOUND?

How many prizes would you win if you had every combination in the Lotto 6/49 draw?

259,139.

That breaks down into one jackpot, six combinations of five out of six numbers drawn with the bonus number, 252 combinations of five out of six numbers drawn without the bonus number, 13,550 combinations of four out of six numbers drawn, and 245,330 combinations of three out of six numbers drawn.

The payout on 259,139 winning tickets would depend on how many other people had winning tickets. Most financial advisers would not advocate covering your bets this way as a good investment strategy, however. The cost of buying enough tickets to cover all combinations is $13,983,816.

How many jewels are in the Queen's crown?

Queen Elizabeth has two crowns. Which one she wears depends on the event she is attending. The smaller crown is the Imperial State Crown; it is the more commonly seen of the two. The Imperial State Crown is worn for such official occasions as the opening of Parliament. This crown has 3,337 precious and semiprecious stones in it, and weighs two pounds, 15 ounces.

The St. Edward's Crown is worn only for coronations. This crown has 440 precious and semiprecious stones in it, and is made mainly of gold. The St. Edward's Crown weighs four pounds, 15 ounces.

Why are curling championships called briars?

The National Briar takes its name from the briar bush, but only in a roundabout manner.

The briar, or brier, is an evergreen of the heath family and is native to Europe. Its root is knobby and is used to make tobacco pipes. A brierroot pipe is also called a briar.

In 1927, Macdonald's Tobacco Company began sponsoring the National Playdowns. One of the company's products was plug tobacco, sold under the trade name of Briar, from the name of the pipe. Macdonald's plugged its plug tobacco by calling the playdowns the Briar.

Macdonald's sponsored the Briar until 1980, when the firm was sold to another tobacco company. The new company pulled out of the game and a new sponsor was found. The new sponsor agreed to keep the name Briar, and the term has virtually become generic.

Macdonald's Tobacco Company also sponsored provincial curling championships, known as Consuls. These tournaments were named after another Macdonald's product, Consul cigarettes.

Why is household dust grey?

Household dust is made up of many types of particles, including bits of dead skin, mite droppings, and lint from clothing. If you could inspect each speck individually, you would see that dust, especially the lint component, comes in a variety of colours.

When the multi-coloured particles gather behind the refrigerator or on the top shelf, the mixture is random. The human eye cannot distinguish the particles individually, so it sees the colours as a blend. Unless one type of dust, such as sawdust or paint dust, predominates, the blend will appear grey.

This principle can be demonstrated by a device called Newton's wheel. This is a disk that has the colours of the spectrum arranged on it like the slices of a pie. When Newton's wheel is spun so fast that your eye can't distinguish the slices, its multi-coloured surface appears to turn one colour: grey.

What is the difference between ice cream and ice milk?

Ice cream is legally required by Consumer and Corporate Affairs Canada to contain at least 10 percent milk fat. Ice milk has between three and a half and five percent milk fat. A product with less than three and a half percent milk fat is merely a "frozen desert."

Milk fat is an essential component of ice cream. It is milk fat that gives ice cream its smooth consistency and rich taste. But a larger component of ice cream is air. One litre of regular ice cream contains about 50 percent air. Gourmet ice cream contains up to 75 percent ice cream and only 25 percent air. Generally speaking, the cheaper the ice cream, the higher the ratio of air to ice cream.

How did the letters of the alphabet get ordered?

The alphabet of most western languages, including English, have their roots in the Old Semitic, or Hebrew, alphabet. The Phoenician alphabet evolved from the Old Semitic alphabet and was subsequently adapted by the Greeks. The Roman alphabet is in turn based on the Greek alphabet. Most of the letters in the English alphabet (and their forms) are from the Roman alphabet. The alphabet gets its name from *alpha* and *beta*, the first two letters of the Greek alphabet.

As these and other languages developed, the names and forms of the letters have changed. However, the order of the letters, as established by the Hebrews, has remained virtually constant. In the Hebrew language, there are no numerals. Instead, the letters of the Hebrew alphabet do double duty by representing number values as well. The first letter, *aleth*, also means one. *Beth*, the second letter, means two, and so on. Since the Hebrew alphabet is also used for counting, the order of the letters is very important. Although later languages used separate numerals to represent numbers, the letters of the alphabet kept their sequence.

How is oil from cars recycled?

The word "recycled" is not widely used in the oil business. Most often, old oil is either re-refined or reclaimed. The difference between the two is the manner in which the oil is processed after recovery.

Oil that is to be re-refined is treated as if it were fresh from the well. This oil is completely re-processed, and is given the same additives as those put into new oil. There can be problems with re-refined oil, however. The oil can become contaminated by other substances such as transmission fluid when it is collected in the garage. If this problem is not caught, it will lead to a substandard batch. Recycled oil that is labelled S.G./C.D. (which means grade G for gas engines and grade D for diesel engines) has been certified by the Automobile Petroleum Institute to meet new car standards.

Oil that is reclaimed is treated with a strong acid. The acid dissolves the dirt and metal fragments in the old oil, but does not affect the oil itself. If a can of oil says recycled, it usually means reclaimed.

According to the Automobile Protection Agency, re-refined oil is better for cars than is reclaimed oil. Volatile elements that are not removed from reclaimed oil will be burned off in the engine, which can lead to mechanical problems. As well, re-refined oil is lighter than reclaimed oil and is therefore a better lubricant.

According to most automobile manufacturers, both reclaimed and re-refined oils are acceptable for their cars, although use of these oils may affect new car warranties. The fine print is usually found in the owner's manual.

What happens to a bullet shot into the air?

In some parts of the world, guns are fired into the air during celebrations. These bullets eventually fall back to the ground, but they are not as dangerous as you might think.

British ballistics expert R.L. Tippins conducted experiments in 1910 to find out what happens to bullets shot vertically. His experiments took place on a beach during low tide. Sixty machine-gun bullets were fired straight up. Fifty to sixty seconds later, the bullets hit the mud 100 to 200 yards away from the gun. Tippins calculated that on average, the bullets rose to about 9000 feet within 19 seconds, then fell back to the earth in 36 seconds.

Later, further experiments were conducted to find out how dangerous these falling bullets could be. One such experiment was set up similarly to Tippins', but with pine boards placed where the bullets would land. The bullets that struck the wood made hardly a mark. From these tests, it was concluded that the return speed of bullets was about 300 feet per second. Given the low weight of a bullet, this corresponds to 30 foot pounds of energy. The British military has determined that twice that energy is required to cause a disabling wound.

A falling bullet therefore has the same impact as a small stone dropped from a great height. However, a bullet fired at an angle of less than 45 degrees from its target is just as deadly as a bullet fired directly at its target.

Why do we throw confetti at weddings?

Throwing confetti, those little bits of coloured paper that have become the bane of priests and church ministers everywhere, is a relatively new wedding tradition.

The practice began in Italy, where confetti is a type of candy. Candy confetti is thrown around during Italian carnivals and spring festivals. This is also where the modern practice of throwing candy to the crowds along a parade route comes from.

Before throwing confetti was in vogue, people attending weddings used to throw rice. The tradition of throwing rice comes to us from the far east, where rice was a symbol of the goddess of fertility. To throw rice at the bride and groom was to wish them many children. Europeans adopted the tradition of throwing rice in the late middle ages.

Throwing confetti in the form of candy-coloured paper at the bride and groom began in England in about 1895 as an alternative to rice.

Most churches view confetti as litter and no longer permit it on their grounds. Rice is also frowned upon because it is dangerous to some birds if consumed. Some churches recommend that wedding guests throw other cereal grains instead.

WHY DO WE THROW CONFETTI AT WEDDINGS?

Why does the Canadian military say "lef-tenant" instead of "loo-tenant?"

Lieutenant is a French word that refers to someone who substitutes for, or takes the place of, a superior officer. "Lieu" means "place " and "tenant" means "holding." The Canadian pronunciation, which comes from the British, is from the old French spelling, *leuftenant*.

The French changed the spelling of the word in the 1700s, and the British followed suit. There were efforts to update the British pronunciation as well, but the traditional "lef-tenant" prevailed. This was also about the time of the American Revolution, which was followed by lingering anti-British, pro-French sentiment in the United States.

Since it was during this period that Americans were adopting spellings and pronunciations different from those of the British for many words, "loo-tenant" became the proper American pronunciation. Changes to British spellings and pronunciations were made permanent with the publication of Noah Webster's American dictionary in 1828.

How did the Scud missile get its name?

The Scud is the Soviet-made missile that achieved notoriety during the Persian Gulf War when the weapon was used by Iraq against civilian population centres in Israel and Saudi Arabia.

Although Scud is a rather silly sounding name, it wasn't dreamt up by either the Soviets or the Iraqis. According to the Canadian Department of National Defence, NATO headquarters in Brussels assigns such nicknames to Soviet weapons. The technique of choosing a name simply involves a pencil, a dictionary, and an element of randomness. Some names seem appropriate to the weapon, whereas others seem rather fanciful.

There is one rule to picking names, however. The first letter must be the same for each type of weapon. Thus, Scud, Scimitar, and Sickle are all missiles. Likewise, the Flogger, Foxbat, and Fishbed are fighter aircraft, and the Bear and Bison are both bombers.

The dictionary has several definitions for scud: to glide or skim along easily; rain or snow driven by the wind; a sudden gust of wind; and low, dark, swiftly moving clouds.

What is a plugged nickel and why is it worthless?

There are several stories that explain the plugged nickel and its value. The earliest dates back to the late 17th century, when coins made of nickel were worth more than their face value. Resourceful crooks hollowed out the coins and plugged them with a cheaper metal. The plugged coins, when discovered, were considered to be worthless as currency.

Another theory says the term comes from the practice some mints had of punching holes into less-than-perfectly minted coins. The holes defaced the coins so they could not be put into circulation. Instead, they were melted down to make new coins.

The explanation from the US Mint in Washington, DC is the most colourful. Back in the days of the wild west, so the story goes, gunmen showed off their prowess with a Colt .45 or a Winchester by tossing a coin in the air and shooting a hole through it. The coin was no longer legal tender once it had been plugged by a gunslinger, so it was worthless. But who's going to argue with an hombre carrying a six-iron and a pocketful of plugged nickels?

Where does the water go when the tide is out?

The tides that go out from the east coast of Canada are not rising on the west coast of Europe. Tides are caused by the gravitational pull of the moon and the sun, as well as the earth's rotation. These forces combine to create circular currents in each of the oceans. There are many such currents in each ocean. These currents rotate and tilt according to the forces acting on them. When the tide is out on the east coast, the water is rising on the opposite edge of that particular tidal current.

The effect of some tidal currents is stronger than others. The world's largest tide is in the Bay of Fundy in New Brunswick, where the difference between high and low tides is more than 15 metres at the head of the bay. On the other end of the scale, the tide in a glass of water is very small.

What are Ps and Qs, and why do they need minding?

These days, "mind your Ps and Qs" is a warning to be on your best behaviour, or at least exercise restraint. But the term originally was much more specific.

In the 17th and 18th centuries, bartenders and barmaids in English alehouses were told to mind their pints and quarts—Ps and Qs; that is, to keep an eye on the stock. Then as now, beer was sold in pint and quart servings. If the staff was too generous when pouring customers' drinks, the establishment would lose profits.

In the days when type was prepared for printing by arranging raised metal letters by hand, printers were warned to mind their Ps and Qs, literally. Since the letters the typesetters arranged were reversed (like those on a rubber stamp), the letters p and q were easily confused.

Why do cartoon characters have only three fingers?

Prior to the development of the animated cartoon, most cartoonists drew their figures with the usual four fingers and a thumb on each hand. The art of cartoon drawing before the 1920s was relatively realistic, although with humorous exaggeration. Originally, a cartoon was merely a preliminary sketch for a more serious work of art.

As cartoonists moved further away from representing an exaggerated view of the real world and towards a representation of a fantasy world, they made up their own rules of anatomy, biology, and physics. Animal characters became more anthropomorphic, or human. As an example, consider famous animal cartoon characters. Peter Rabbit and Rupert the Bear are from the old school; Bugs Bunny and Yogi Bear represent the new approach.

With the introduction of the animated cartoon, many cartoonists became more interested in how their new characters would move in the new fantasy world. For the animator, it is easier and more convincing to make three sausage-like fingers move than it is to make four full-articulated fingers bend realistically. Characters were made rounder and more rubbery; the fourth finger disappeared to make room for the more balloon-like digits.

The three-fingered character is a convention, not a rule. Many cartoonists with a more realistic style still draw four fingers. But even within the same cartoon, the number of fingers on each character's hand can vary. In Walt Disney's *Snow White*, for example, the title character has four fingers on each hand, while the cartoony dwarfs have three stubby fingers per hand.

WHY DO CARTOON CHARACTERS HAVE ONLY
THREE FINGERS?

Why is the name Gordon Bennett used as a curse?

"Gordon Bennett!" is a mild, euphemistic expletive, about on par with "God Almighty!" It comes from a newspaper publisher who was adept at sparking angry responses from the church community.

James Gordon Bennett was born in Scotland in 1795. He was from a Catholic family and trained for the priesthood. At age 24, he abandoned his career plans and came to North America, where he worked in Halifax, Boston, and Charleston as a teacher and translator. He eventually found a job as a reporter in New York.

Bennett started his own newspaper, the New York *Herald*, in 1835. Just as Orson Welles did in *Citizen Kane*, Bennett outlined his policy in his first issue. Bennett wrote: "We shall support no party, be the agent of no faction or coterie, and care nothing for any election or candidate, from President down to constable." That independent attitude made the *Herald* exceptional.

Bennett knew how to peddle his papers. He said he believed that the job of a newspaper was "not to instruct but to startle." His paper was full of vivid accounts of fires, murders, public love affairs, and financial scandals. The coverage of these stories outraged the sensibilities of church leaders and other pillars of the community. Bennett's name came to express the moral outrage felt by these upstanding citizens toward his paper.

The *Herald* was more than just a scandal sheet, however. It was the first American paper to post foreign correspondents in Europe. Bennett also assigned 63 reporters to cover the Civil War.

Bennett had a son who inherited both his name and his love of the newspaper game. Bennett Jr. sent the journalist and explorer Henry Morton Stanley to Africa to search for a lost missionary. Their encounter gave us the phrase, "Dr. Livingston, I presume?"

Why is Toronto's NHL team called the Maple Leafs and not the Maple Leaves?

Because Conn Smythe and the *Globe and Mail* said so.

Toronto's was one of the original teams when the National Hockey League was formed in 1917. The team, then called the Arenas, was the first NHL team to win the Stanley Cup. The Arenas changed their name to the St. Patricks in 1919. The St. Pats, as they were also known, made it to the Cup finals but lost in 1921 and 1922, then won in the 1922-23 season.

In 1927, a group of Toronto businessmen purchased the St. Pats. Among those businessmen was Conn Smythe, who became the team's coach and manager the following season.

According to the Hockey Hall of Fame, it was Smythe who gave the team its new name. Smythe later wrote that the new name was better because it would mean something to all Canadians. He noted that the members of the Canadian Olympic team of 1924 wore maple leaf crests on their chests, and that he had worn the maple leaf on badges and insignia on his uniform during the First World War. St. Patricks, according to Smythe, was "a name hatched originally merely in an attempt to attract the Irish population of Toronto."

There is no official record stating why the team is called the Leafs rather than the Leaves. However, the reason given by the Hockey Hall of Fame is that Smythe said it would be that way because it sounds better. The new, orthographically eccentric name didn't take long to catch on. The team was purchased on the evening of February 14th; the sub-head to the story in the next day's *Globe and Mail* read, "Goodbye, St. Pats! Howdy, Maple Leafs."

Smythe continued as general manager of the Toronto Maple Leafs until the 1956-57 season. Over that 20-year period, the Leafs played in 14 final matches, winning the Stanley Cup seven times.

When did the practice of preserving food in tin cans begin?

Sealing food in tin cans for commercial purposes began in France in 1809. The principle was simple—food was heated to destroy anything that could spoil it and then was sealed in an air-tight container. Free from bacterial contamination, food lasted indefinitely and tasted just as good when the can was pried open.

Although the early ideas about destroying bacteria by heating were valid, there were problems with early canning practices. In the 1800s, tin cans were sealed with solder, an alloy of tin and lead. Lead is a poison that affects the brain. Lethargy and poor judgement are among the symptoms of lead poisoning. Many people died from eating food tainted with lead that had leached from the seams of the can into the food. The ill-fated Franklin expedition, for example, is believed to have succumbed to lead poisoning from its food supply. The expedition left England in 1845 for the Canadian Arctic with a massive supply of canned food. Experiments on the exhumed bodies of the crew members and research at their gravesites suggest they all fell victim to lead poisoning.

Where does the superstition of knocking on wood come from?

Many cultures revered trees, believing them to be inhabited by good spirits. Knocking on wood was a ritual when seeking the favours of these tree-dwelling beings.

The Celts of ancient Britain believed that if they wanted a favour from the spirits, they would have to touch the bark of the tree in which the spirits lived while the request was made. If the wish was granted, the person was to return to the tree and knock on it three times as an expression of thanks.

Knocking on wood after a boast was practiced by Greeks, Egyptians, Germans, and North American Indians. They believed that boasting about one's good fortune would make the gods jealous, and that boasting of future accomplishments was a sure guarantee that they would never happen. Knocking on wood was a quick way of seeking divine forgiveness before the damage was done.

Ideas for the best wood for knocking varied among cultures. Both North American Indians and ancient Greeks were particularly fond of oak. They noticed that oak trees were frequently struck by lightning, and so thought the sky gods lived in those trees. The Dutch thought the type of wood didn't matter, as long as it was unvarnished, unpainted, and uncarved.

Why are lobsters cooked alive?

Raw lobster meat, and that of any crustacean, begins to deteriorate so quickly after death that it poses a serious health risk. Even though cooking kills the bacteria in the dead meat, the toxins the bacteria produce are heat-stable and will still be present after cooking. Consequently, it is illegal under fish inspection regulations to cook dead crustaceans.

This does not mean dead lobsters cannot be sold; it only means that the dead lobsters must have been cooked alive.

This is what to look for if you suspect your lobster was not alive and kicking when it was cooked, according to the Prince Edward Island Department of Fisheries and Oceans. The meat in a cooked lobster should be long and stringy. Because of the rapid decomposition that breaks down the meat, the strings in the tail meat of a lobster cooked after it is already dead are short, like grains of rice. Inspectors call this "short meat."

If a lobster is cooked alive, the tail curls because of reflex action. A dead lobster has no reflexes, so its tail remains straight.

Rapid decomposition also causes an unpleasant odour that is a dead giveaway that the lobster was not cooked alive.

WHY ARE LOBSTERS COOKED ALIVE?

Where did the 1960s peace symbol come from?

The peace symbol conjures up images of Haight-Ashbury, bellbottoms, and acidheads, but it actually predates the 1960s. The symbol was first used during an anti-nuclear demonstration organised by the British Ban the Bomb Movement in 1958.

The movement was opposed to US bases and hydrogen bomb factories on British soil. Although the peace symbol is associated with the hippie era, the British Ban the Bomb Movement was hardly inspired by youthful rebellion. Its founders were Canon John Collins of St. Paul's Cathedral and philosopher Bertrand Russell.

The symbol overlaps two letters in semaphore code. The inverted V shape, with the semaphore flags at the 4 o'clock and 8 o'clock positions, stands for the letter N. The vertical line, with the flags at 12 o'clock and 6 o'clock, stands for the letter D. ND is an abbreviation for Nuclear Disarmament.

Why is the car that carries coffins called a hearse?

"Hearse" comes from the Latin word *hirpex*, which means a rake or harrow. In medieval times, the coffins of distinguished citizens were decorated with candles. These candles were supported by a spiked frame, which looked like a rake with its spikes pointing upwards. The spiked frame was called a hearse.

The French modified the frame so that it could support the coffin as it was was carried by pallbearers to the church service and then to the graveyard. Wheels were later added to the framework, turning the coffin into its own wagon. When a separate wagon carrying coffins became part of the funeral ritual, it was called a hearse. The name was passed on to the motorized vehicles that carry coffins today.

Who is the man on Canadian Tire money?

The man with the handlebar moustache and curly white hair, wearing a plaid scarf and a feathered fur tam, is Sandy McTire. He represents traditional Scottish frugality on behalf of the Canadian Tire retailing chain. His image is on every bill of Canadian Tire money.

The coupons were introduced in the mid-1960s as an incentive to get the chain's gas station customers into its department stores. The coupons were handed out at the gas bars, but were good only for merchandise purchased in the stores.

Sandy McTire was designed by former Manager of Store Planning, Bernie Freedman. The coupons are made from authentic currency paper, with the same rag content and spot marks as legal tender. At any time, there is about $20 million in Canadian Tire money, if not exactly in circulation, in glove compartments and cupboards across the country.

Why do Rice Krispies snap, crackle, and pop?

According to the Consumer Services Office of Kellogg's, this is the most frequently asked question they get. When rice kernels are toasted, a network of tiny air pockets develops inside them. These pockets cause milk to be absorbed unevenly inside the krispie. Once the milk is added, the krispie expands. Since different parts of the krispie expand at different rates, the air pockets break under the strain, causing the familiar snap, crackle, and pop.

Kellogg's introduced Rice Krispies to the market in 1928, but the snap, crackle, and pop were not part of the original marketing strategy. Somehow, the characteristic sound was overlooked by the research and development department. The sound effects were first highlighted in the advertising and packaging in 1932. The characters Snap, Crackle, and Pop started pitching the product in 1940.

Who created the bikini?

The two-piece bathing suit is named after Bikini Atoll, part of the Marshall Islands chain in the Pacific Ocean. It was there in 1946 that the United States was preparing to test some of its new atomic bombs.

Meanwhile, French designer Louis Reard, creator of the two-piece bathing suit, was making plans to reveal his rather revealing new creation to the fashion world. The only problem was that he didn't have a name for the swimsuit. With a bit of inspired marketing savvy, Reard exploited the publicity surrounding the upcoming atomic testing to his own advantage. He dropped his own bombshell on the world, calling it the bikini.

The US detonated its atomic bomb on July 1, 1946, and the bikini was dropped on the fashion world of Paris four days later to at least as much controversy.

What is the origin of the Celtic cross?

The Celtic cross, a cross overlapping a circle, is also known as the high cross of Ireland. The circle represents eternity, with no beginning and no end. The cross, of course, represents Christ. Together, the cross and the circle refer to the eternal God subjecting himself to the limits of time and humanity.

The design dates back to the fifth century, during the time of St. Patrick, the patron saint of Ireland. According to legend, the communion plate had been stolen from St. Patrick's church's altar. St. Assicus prayed for the plate's return. In miraculous answer to his prayer, a golden plate floated down from heaven and landed on the altar. On the plate was imprinted the Celtic cross.

Once they had the design, the Celts of ancient Ireland erected huge crosses, some up to 18 feet tall, across the country to mark holy places such as abbeys and the burial places of great kings. Crosses were also illustrated, to teach people about the Bible. There are still 72 of the crosses standing today in Ireland.

The first crosses used as markers were made of metal. Between the eighth and twelfth centuries, stonemasons took over the responsibility of building Celtic crosses.

What is the origin of Ground Hog Day?

What today we call Ground Hog Day started as a celebration for the Virgin Mary called Candlemas. Candlemas Day is a Roman Catholic festival that began in Europe during the middle ages. The second day of February is still called Candlemas Day in Europe.

According to European tradition, if a hedgehog came out of winter hibernation on Candlemas Day and saw its shadow, there would be six more weeks of winter. When the European settlers brought the tradition with them to North America, they changed the hedgehog into a groundhog, owing to the absence of hedgehogs on this continent.

The native tribes of North America also had a tradition based on the groundhog. According to legend, a groundhog named Nawgeentuck saved the life of a Mohawk called Klionda during a winter storm. Klionda believed that the groundhog was a gift from the Great Spirit, and that the groundhog had the power to ensure the survival of human life.

Another native tradition called for tribal chiefs to mark the end of winter by capturing a groundhog and cooking it in a stew. This was the time when the blood of groundhogs was beleived to have purifying powers, and so was the only time it was permissible to eat groundhogs.

WHAT IS THE ORIGIN OF GROUNDHOG DAY?

When did the military tradition of saluting originate?

Saluting goes back to the days of knights in armour. Prior to this, soldiers showed their respect to superior officers by removing their headgear. It wasn't practical, however, to do the same with a knight's helmet—getting it on in the first place was trouble enough. Instead, the knights simply raised a hand upwards toward their heads. The palm was turned outward to show there was no weapon hidden.

Over the years, the salute has been changed by different military branches of many countries to give each branch its own individual touch. The different styles caused a problem for Canada's military when the forces were unified in 1968. Prior to that time, the Royal Canadian Air Force, Navy and Army each had their own salutes. The Canadian Armed Forces settled on a salute similar to the naval style, with the palm almost parallel to the ground.

Who invented the baby bottle?

Babies have been fed milk from bottles since classical Greek times. The first bottles were urns with two openings. One opening was used for filling the urn, and the other, shaped like a beak, was stuffed with a piece of rolled cloth, such as linen. The cloth absorbed the milk and served as a nipple.

Many materials have been used in the search for the perfect nipple. Nipples have been made from silver, pewter, leather, ivory, wood, and pickled cow's teat. The India rubber nipple was patented in the United States in 1845, and the modern rubber nipple was introduced in 1930 in England.

The disposable bottle was developed in Canada and was introduced in 1960.

How do fish see in the depths of the ocean?

Some fish can see where they are going down to a depth of about a kilometre. There is still sufficient sunlight shining through the water for fish to see at that depth. These fish have retinas at the back of their eyeballs that are made of several layers of rod-shaped cells. The rod cells are sensitive to the faintest light, but limit the fish's vision to black and white.

Many fish that live in water deeper than one kilometre produce their own light. Enzymes in special organs of the fish produce this light. Lantern fish have these organs right beside their eyes, operating like headlights.

Not all deep-sea fish can see, however. Some are blind, so they rely on other senses to survive. These fish have nerve endings in groupings called lateral lines. The lateral lines sense the movement in the water of other creatures.

Most blind fish are found at depths of four to five kilometres, and some have been discovered eight kilometres below the surface. Blindness is an adaptation that benefits the fish that live deep in the water. It takes more energy to see than it does to feel, hear, or smell, and food is very scarce that deep. A sighted fish would probably not be able to locate enough food to replenish the energy it used looking for the food in the first place.

Why is the boxing ring called a ring when it's square?

Boxing rings may be square today, but they haven't always been so. The sport of boxing probably began with the ancient Greeks and Romans. In those days, boxers drew a circle on the ground and fought within that boundary. When boxing began its comeback in the 1700s, boxers still drew a circle on the ground, but this time they added a line through the middle of the circle. Each round ended when one boxer was knocked to the ground, but as long as he could make it back to his side of the line, the match would continue. The expressions "toe the line" and "come up to the mark" come from this practice.

Boxing was becoming more organized in Britain at about this time. Bare-knuckled prize fighters fought on circular platforms called rings or booths. When the platforms were moved from the outdoors to indoor locations, they were raised about five feet so that the audience could more easily follow the action. A fence was added to the perimeter of the platform so fighters couldn't fall off.

The square ring was introduced in 1839. According to the London Prize Ring rules, the ring was 24 feet square. The round shape was changed to a square so that boxers would have definite corners where they could confer with their trainers, and so that there could be a clear neutral space between opposite corners.

What is the difference between a violin and a fiddle?

Although "fiddle" is usually used as a slang term for violin, to the musician there is an important distinction between the two. Each instrument is adapted to the type of music played on it.

The bodies of a violin and fiddle are the same, but the two are strung differently. The strings of a fiddle are set flatter at the bridge than are those on a violin, while the strings of a violin have a higher arch at the bridge so that they may be played further up the neck of the instrument. The strings of a violin must not be pressed beyond a certain point, otherwise the fingers may interfere with other strings. Therefore, the middle strings of a violin must be set higher than on a fiddle to make them accessible.

The strings of a fiddle are usually made of steel, while the strings of a violin are made of gut or a synthetic product similar to gut. The sound of steel string is sharp compared to the smooth sound of gut string, which is one reason why Don Messer sounds different from Itzak Perlman.

Why don't bears' muscles atrophy during hibernation?

Human muscles will atrophy, or get weaker, if they are not used. This can be a problem for bed-ridden hospital patients, or for anyone with a broken limb in a cast.

Hibernating bears are in a different situation. During winter, they have "carnivore lethargy." This means that, although they're in deep sleep, they are not completely dormant. During hibernation, bears shift around and turn over in their sleep. This movement is enough to keep their muscles working

During hibernation, a bear's metabolic rate is so low that it can survive on its fatty tissue alone. Bears do, however, lose their muscle tone over the winter. That is why bear meat is best in the spring, when the muscle is softest.

Yet it looks like this isn't the whole story. Scientists suspect there is also an unidentified enzyme at work in hibernating bears, preventing muscle atrophy. Researchers hope to isolate this enzyme and give it to humans with degenerative muscle and bone diseases.

WHY DON'T BEARS' MUSCLES ATROPHY
DURING HIBERNATION?

What is the origin of the expression "the life of Reilly"?

To live the life of Reilly is to live the good life. The phrase comes from a song from the 1880s about a saloonkeeper who was so successful that he was able to raise his establishment to the dignity of a hotel.

The song, called *Are You the O'Reilly*, was made popular by the vaudevillian Pat Rooney. At the end of each verse sung by Rooney, the audience would sing the chorus:

Are you the O'Reilly who keeps this hotel,
Are you the O'Reilly they speak of so well,
Are you the the O'Reilly they speak of so highly,
Gorblimey, O'Reilly, you're looking well.

The Life of Reilly was also the title of a radio and television program that ran through the 1940s and '50s. The situation comedy starred William Bendix as the beleaguered head of his household. For one season, Bendix was replaced by a newcomer who went on to live the live of Reilly himself, Jackie Gleason.

Why are pistachio nuts dyed red?

The shells of pistachio nuts are naturally light brown. Yet some of them are red by the time they hit the supermarket.

Pistachios must be dried before they can be sent to market. In the 1930s, nuts imported from Turkey and Iran were very often left to dry in the sun too long. Moisture became trapped in the hull of the nut, causing it to stain the shell a dark brown. This staining did not affect the taste of the pistachio, but the colour was unappealing to the North American market. Dyeing the nuts red masked the brown and increased the saleability of the product.

Pistachio nuts are also grown in California. These nuts are dried by a mechanical process. The shells of these nuts are a more appetizing shade of sandy brown. Most of the nuts produced in California are left their natural colour; however, red is still the preferred colour in the eastern United States. Red pistachios are also more common during the Christmas season.

Canadians also prefer red pistachios, but the market is changing. In the past, 80 per cent of pistachio nuts sold in Canada were dyed red. Today, only 60 per cent are dyed red.

What's that stuff they use to de-ice airplanes?

Aircraft that require de-icing are sprayed with a mixture of water and ethylene glycol, which is an alcohol with a low freezing point. The mixture, which is heated to 180 degrees Fahrenheit before application, prevents ice from forming on the airplane's wings. The ratio of water to glycol usually depends on the weather, although some airports keep their supply of the mixture at a concentration adequate for all temperatures.

If the weather is cold enough, de-icing may be unnecessary. If the temperature and humidity are low enough, there is little risk of ice forming on the wings. De-icing is essential during periods of freezing rain or wet snow, however. De-icing a plane costs five hundred to five thousand dollars, depending on the size of the plane and the weather.

The airplane's crew and airport maintenance people confer with each other before a plane is de-iced, but the final decision to de-ice or not is made by the captain.

When did the Scottish tradition of First Footing originate?

First Footing is the second half of a Scottish New Year's tradition that dates back to Celtic times.

The first half of the New Year's celebration is called Hogmanay. On the last day of the year, Scots clean up the old year's business so they can start fresh in the new year. Debts are paid up, enemies are forgiven, and houses are swept. The hearth is cleaned of old ashes and a new fire is lit.

First Footing begins at midnight, when everyone visits neighbours and exchanges gifts. According to tradition, the first person over your doorstep indicated the luck you'd have in the new year. A dark-haired man was an omen of a good year. A fair-haired person of either sex, on the other hand, was symbolic of Vikings on the rampage, which meant anything but good luck to the early Scots.

The Scottish New Year's traditions are still honoured, often with a party that begins at midnight and continues until daylight, with more guests dropping in for breakfast.

How long has the Leaning Tower of Pisa been leaning?

The Leaning Tower of Pisa began leaning even before its construction was completed, and it is now about four and a half metres off the plumb line. Construction of the tower was begun in 1174. It was built on soil that was sandy, and the water table at the time was very high. Halfway through construction, the water table dropped and the soil shifted, causing the tower to lean.

The project was left uncompleted for almost two centuries. When construction resumed in 1370, the new builder planned the remaining portion of the job so that the weight of the new part of the building disguised the lean of the old. It did not, however, stop the tower from continuing to lean.

The tower continues to tilt a little bit more each year—in 1989, the tower shifted by another two millimetres. According to the Italian government, the tower has to shift another 48 millimetres, or about one degree, before it tumbles over. The government has hired a construction company to shore up the tower before it collapses. The company plans to take the tower down piece by piece and put it back together. The Italian government is looking for United Nations help to finance the job, which it is estimated will cost US$500 million.

Why is the Olympic motto in Latin and not Greek?

The modern Olympic movement was inspired by the Olympic Games of ancient Greece, which were in turn named for Mount Olympus, home of the Greek gods. Yet the Olympic motto, *citius altius fortius*, which means "swifter higher stronger," is in Latin.

Baron Pierre de Coubertin, who revived the Olympics in 1894, wanted to improve the education system in France. He felt that including sports in the curriculum would train students to work harder to accomplish their other goals in life. With this idea in mind, the Baron visited one of his friends, a priest who ran a school for middle- and upper-class boys. De Coubertin noticed a slogan carved above the school door. It read *citius altius fortius*, and seemed to fit his Olympic idea perfectly.

At the time, Latin was much more widely studied than Greek, so a slogan in Latin would more likely be understood.

In June 1894, Pierre de Coubertin founded the International Olympic Committee, and one month later the motto appeared, in the original Latin, on the masthead of the first IOC bulletin. The motto stuck, and has been inspiring athletes ever since.

Why do only female mosquitoes feed on blood?

Only female mosquitoes feed on blood. Male mosquitoes are vegetarians, making do with nectar from flowering plants.

Female mosquitoes will feed on the blood of almost any animal, as long as they are able to get it. The list of preferred victims is determined more by access than by taste.

The best victims are large mammals, such as cattle, deer, and humans. These animals are easily located by the heat they radiate. Smaller mammals and birds are next on the hit list. These animals, especially their young, have coats thin enough to be easily pierced. Chicks are particularly susceptible to mosquito bites because they have thin skin, no feathers for protection, and cannot escape their nests.

If none of these sources of food is available, a mosquito will get quite resourceful. Scientists have even found garter snakes infected with the same mosquito-borne sleeping sickness that plagues humans.

If there is absolutely no animal life available, a female mosquito will resort to feeding on the same nectar that the male mosquitos feed on all the time.

Female mosquitos feed on blood because of the proteins found in blood plasma. Without these proteins in its diet, the female mosquito is unable to produce eggs that will develop properly.

WHY DO ONLY FEMALE MOSQUITOS FEED ON BLOOD?

What was the first television commercial?

Announcements from sponsors began interrupting television programs within minutes of commercial television going on the air. But the evolution of television took a long time, and the first experiments in television date back to the earliest days of radio.

The Radio Corporation of America, more commonly known as RCA, set up the first radio network in 1926. This network was the National Broadcasting Corporation, NBC. RCA was very active in broadcasting research, since company president David Sarnoff recognized that better radios meant bigger radio audiences for NBC's programming.

RCA was also heavily involved in the development of television broadcasting. The first experimental television station was W2XBS, set up by RCA in New York in 1928. The first signals were very fuzzy, as they consisted of 48 horizontal lines, as compared to the 525 lines of today, or the 1150 lines of high-definition television. One of those test broadcasts, in 1930, was of a toy figure of Felix the Cat set on a record turntable, which makes the newspaper strip character the first case of media crossover to television.

CBS, which began as a radio network in 1928, began its television broadcasts in 1931 with an appearance by both New York Mayor Jimmy Walker and Kate Smith, who sang *When the Moon Comes Over the Mountain.* Among the network's other experimental programming was coverage of the presidential election of 1932.

By 1937, there were a few thousand TV sets receiving images from 17 experimental stations, none of which were permitted to run commercials to support their efforts. Programming included plays, such as *Susan and God,* starring Gertrude Lawrence, shown in 1938. The first sports telecast was a baseball game between Princeton and Columbia on May 17, 1939. The camera has such a restricted field of view that it had to be swung back and forth between the pitcher's mound and home plate to catch the action.

Incidentally, Princeton won the game, 2-1, in the tenth inning.

General broadcasting for home viewing began in 1939. Sarnoff chose April 30, 1939 for the inaugural program. The star of the show was President Franklin D. Roosevelt; the scene was the official opening of the New York World's Fair.

W2XBS was granted the first commercial licence by the Federal Communications Commission in the spring of 1941. The station's call letters were changed to WNBT, and July 1, 1941 was set as the first day of commercial broadcasting. The broadcast day began with the time, temperature, and weather. There were three 15-minute programs: the news with Lowell Thomas, a simulcast of the radio program *Truth or Consequences*, and *Uncle Jim's Spelling Bee*. The first commercial sportscast, also on that day, was a Dodgers-Pirates game played at Ebbets Field in Brooklyn.

The first commercial, which aired that day, was for Bulova watches. The commercial simply showed the face of a watch and featured an announcer's voiceover. The commercial cost Bulova nine dollars—of course, nine dollars was worth a lot more back then. Other sponsors for that day included Lever Brothers, Proctor & Gamble, and Sun Oil.

Why does polyester fabric develop pills?

Polyester, especially if it is blended with natural fibres, is prone to developing pills, or little balls. Once the pills start, there seems to be no getting rid of them.

Polyester is a synthetic textile made of long, thin filaments that have been woven to produce cloth. Cotton is a natural fabric made of short fibres from the cotton plant that have been woven to produce thread. A poly-cotton blend is manufactured by cutting the polyester filaments to the length of cotton fibres and weaving them together with cotton.

Friction from wear and washing causes the smooth polyester filaments to slip out of the weave and to form little balls. The same process occurs in acrylic products. Better-quality blend garments are made from longer cotton fibres, which hold longer polyester filaments in place.

Attempting to remove pills by pulling on them aggravates the problem by pulling out other fibres that will eventually also roll up into balls. The best way to remove pills is to cut them off with a razor-sharp blade.

Why are there so few calories in aspartame as compared with sugar?

Aspartame is the sugar substitute sold under the brand name Nutrasweet. Because it has a very low caloric content, aspartame is not a source of energy that must be burned off to avoid weight gain. For example, a 12-ounce can of regular soft drink contains 150 to 170 calories, but the diet version of the same drink has only 2 calories because of the aspartame.

Aspartame is a combination of two natural amino acids—aspartic acid and phenylalanine—found in common, protein-rich foods. The two amino acids are digested easily without releasing much energy.

Of course, the appeal of aspartame goes beyond dieting. Because it is not a sugar, aspartame does not promote tooth decay.

Why are bulldozers yellow?

Most construction vehicles are yellow so that they can be easily seen. Yellow is a colour to which the human eye is very sensitive. This is also why fire engines in many cities were changed recently from red to yellow, or yellow-green.

Best and Holt, an industrial vehicle manufacturer, developed the caterpillar tractor in 1925. The colour of these vehicles depended on who bought them. The tractors were brightly coloured for the construction industry and were painted the manufacturer's own colours, grey with red trim, for the agricultural market. In 1932, the company settled on bright yellow for construction vehicles. Best and Holt also registered the name of the colour, caterpillar yellow. The colour has become the industry standard, although other manufacturers, such as Massey Ferguson and John Deere, still use their own company colors for agricultural vehicles.

Why is a police interrogation called "the third degree"?

The third degree is a staple scene in any movie about hard-boiled cops. A confession is extracted from the suspect after hours of bad lighting and worse dialogue. "The third degree" can also refer to any tough questioning.

The term "the third degree" comes from Freemasonry. In that fraternal organization, the third degree, or third level, is Master Mason. The title is given only after a series of elaborate initiation ceremonies.

The term "third degree" as it applies to police methods was first used in about 1911 in Washington, DC. As explained by Washington's police superintendent, Major Richard Sylvester, there are three degrees to law enforcement. The first degree is administered when the police officer makes the arrest, the second degree is the imprisonment of the suspect, and the third degree occurs when the suspect is taken from the jail cell to private quarters for interrogation.

Why are the colours of the second rainbow backwards?

The colours of the rainbow are revealed when sunlight passes through water droplets in the air. The droplets bend the white light, causing it to break up into the individual colours of the spectrum. From the inside of the arc, these colours are red, orange, yellow, green, blue, indigo, and violet. This prism effect is also created by glass, any other reflective surface, or water from a sprinkler.

If there is enough water in the air, and if the sunlight is bright enough, there can be a second rainbow radiating from the first. The colours of this second rainbow are in reverse order. This is because the water droplets in the air are reflecting the first rainbow, creating a mirror image. A mirror image is always backwards compared to the original.

Occasionally, there is even a third rainbow, which is a reflection of the second. This third rainbow is backwards again, which puts the colours back in their original order.

Why do matadors use a red cape when bullfighting?

According to ethologists—scientists who study animal behavior—bulls have very poor visual perception. When a matador's taunts (not to mention the spikes stabbed into its neck) make a bull see red, it's not actually seeing red.

The matador's cape serves two functions. First, it provides a moving target. Because of the bull's limited vision, stationary objects are difficult to differentiate. The cape appears separate from the background because it waves and flows. The red of the cape, while not seen by the bull as a bright colour, also stands out because of its contrast with the duller colours of the ring. But the bull is not provoked specifically by the colour.

Second, the cape misdirects the bull, steering the charging animal around the matador. The skill of the matador is measured by how flamboyantly he can manipulate the bull in this manner.

WHY DO MATADORS USE A RED CAPE WHEN
BULLFIGHTING?

What is the origin of Mother's Day?

The first Mother's Day was celebrated in 1908 in Grafton, West Virginia. The Act honouring mothers with a special day was passed by Congress six years later, after a campaign by a school teacher named Anna Jarvis.

Jarvis was so devoted to her mother that she was uncomfortable even leaving home to attend college. When her mother died, Jarvis felt guilty for not doing what she felt was enough while the older woman was still living. For two years, the daughter was plagued with guilt. Finally, Jarvis asked the Andrews Methodist Sunday School, where her mother taught for 20 years, to hold a special service on the anniversary of her death. The service was to be in honour of all mothers. At the end of the service, Jarvis handed a carnation to each of the children in attendance—a white carnation if the child's mother had passed away, or red if she was still living.

The idea of Mother's Day caught on very quickly with the public. However, when the campaigners approached the lawmakers in Washington, there was some initial resistance within the Senate to creating an officially-recognized Mother's Day. The challenge withered away against continued pressure from the press, the public and the rest of the government. On May 8, 1914, President Woodrow Wilson signed the proclamation that designated the second Sunday in May as Mother's Day.

Despite the success of her campaign, Anna Jarvis did not live a happy life. Partly as a result of her disillusionment with and opposition to the commercialization of Mother's Day, Jarvis became a recluse. She died in 1948 at 85 years of age. At the time, she was broke, deaf, nearly blind, and childless.

How do cats purr?

Cats purr when they are contented. They also purr at just about any other time. That's because the purring sound, unlike meowing, does not come from a voluntary action.

A purr is produced by the vibration of a large vein in a cat's chest cavity. The contraction of diaphragm muscles around this vein restricts the blood flow, creating the vibration. The sound of the vibration is amplified by the bronchial tubes and windpipes. How loud the cat purrs depends on how constricted the vein is at the time.

No one knows for sure why cats purr, but one theory relates to kittens. Newborn kittens have no sense of smell, and their ears are underdeveloped. However, they are able to feel the vibration of their mother's purring and can use it as a homing signal.

Why is hot water from a hotel room tap instantly hot?

Hotel water is hot right from the tap because, unlike water at home, it does not have to come from a water heater elsewhere in the building. Hotels have a recirculating system that provides a constant supply of hot water to their fixtures. The recirculating system has a small electric heater and an extra pipe close to each room. When the hot water tap is turned on, water comes from this pipe for a few seconds until the main water system is able to provide hot water.

Providing this convenience to guests actually saves hotels money, since it prevents gallons of water from being wasted every time a guest waits for water from the tap to get hot.

What is the purpose of a humidex reading?

The humidex reading is just another way of saying "it isn't the heat, it's the humidity." A humidex reading is an adjustment to the daily temperature to account for the the effect humidity has on the body's ability to cool itself. During summer, humid air feels warmer than dry air because it is harder for the body to cool down by evaporating sweat.

A humidex reading is a combination of the dewpoint temperature and the outside temperature. The dewpoint is the temperature at which water vapour in the air condenses into liquid. If the atmospheric temperature drops to the dewpoint, the result is fog.

Environment Canada has a scale that relates the humidex reading to how comfortable one feels. The comfortable range is 20 to 29 degrees. At 30 to 39 degrees, there are "varying degrees of uncomfortability," and 40 to 45 degrees is uncomfortable. Labour Canada restricts outdoor work when the humidex reading exceeds 45 degrees.

Why don't the Governor-General and his wife have to pay the GST?

The Governor-General and his wife represent the Crown in Canada. Since the Crown does not pay taxes to itself, the Governor-General is exempt from paying the Goods and Services Tax (GST) for anything that is bought for official government business.

Much of the Governor-General's business requires that he include his wife, so her purchases are GST-exempt as well. To make shopping convenient they carry an exemption card, which allows them to make their purchases hassle-free. These purchases can be just about anything—from clothing to home furnishings for the official residence—as long as they are for official use.

The legislation that allows the Governor-General to be exempt from the GST is in the Excise Tax Act under Part 8, called Zero-Rated Supplies. The exemption has been there since 1916 and also applied to the old Federal Sales Tax.

How did bureaucratic delay become known as "red tape"?

The term "red tape" comes from the British government, although the practice of bureaucratic delay can be found just about everywhere.

In the 17th century, British government officials and lawyers tied important documents together with red ribbons. The British Houses of Parliament, fond as they were of pomp and drama, made a ceremonious production of tying and untying the red ribbon that bound all important documents. Consequently, the red tape came to symbolize useless legal delay and obsessive adherence to the letter of rules and regulations.

One of the earliest written references to red tape in its derogatory sense came from author Washington Irving, who wrote in 1839, "his brain was little more than red tape and parchment." Poet Henry Wadsworth Longfellow complained in 1869 of spending "all morning at the custom house . . . plagued with red tape."

The British government is no longer encumbered by red tape. These days, official documents are bound together by pink tape.

HOW DID BUREAUCRATIC DELAY BECOME KNOWN AS "RED TADE"?

Why did it take so long for Canada to update the Queen's portrait on our coins?

Back in the pre-Constitutional days of the 1960s and before, effigies for Canadian coins came from Britain. Even now, the coins of Britain's colonies, and many non-colonial Commonwealth members, have the same image as those of Britain.

The proposed design of British coins is submitted to a government committee, then given royal approval. Once accepted, the design is sent to the rest of the Commonwealth. The first design depicting the Queen came after her coronation in 1952. The winning design was chosen by Prince Philip, who is both the Duke of Edinburgh and the Queen's husband. The winning artist was granted sittings with the new monarch to perfect the likeness.

The British mint gave the Queen a more mature image in 1965, and Canadian coins were also changed at that time. Britain again updated the design in 1981, but this time Canada rejected the new look. The Royal Canadian Mint began work on its own updated effigy of the Queen in 1985, using a design by Canadian artist Dora Depedery-Hunt. This design was introduced on coins minted in 1990. This change was at the initiative of the Canadian government, but the final design still required the Queen's approval.

Why do apples turn brown after they've been cut?

A biochemical reaction occurs when oxygen comes into contact with the raw flesh of an apple. The oxygen breaks down components of apple flesh called oxylic compounds, which normally have a neutral pH. When the oxygen breaks down these compounds, it causes them to turn acidic. This process is called enzymatic browning.

When an apple browns, it is attempting to heal its wound by regeneration. Of course, a peeled apple cannot grow a whole new skin, but the process is effective with smaller punctures in the apple skin. The rough scars on some apples, for example, are the result of enzymatic browning, which heals the wounds caused by insects and other animals that feed on the fruit while it is still on the tree.

Exposed apple flesh will not turn brown if it is coated with another acid. Ascorbic acid and citric acid are often used to keep fruit looking fresh. Finally, if you think brown apples are unappetizing, switch to Cortland apples, which do not turn brown.

Why do leaves change colour in the fall?

The leaves of deciduous trees—the trees that shed their leaves in the fall—contain two major kinds of pigments. The first is chlorophyll, the green pigment that the leaves use to capture the sunlight they require for photosynthesis. The second kind of pigment is made up of carotenes, which are similar to the pigments in carrots.

Carotenes, which are red and yellow, are always present in leaves. During summer, chlorophyll predominates and the leaves appear green. When fall comes, however, the chlorophyll starts to degrade, and the leaves change colour. Because the carotenes degrade more slowly than the chlorophyll does, the leaves appear to turn red, yellow, and orange—then brown.

Synthesis of other pigments is triggered by the coming of warm days and cold nights. These pigments, called anthocyanins, turn the leaves red, blue, and purple. The anthocyanins build up and accumulate at different rates from day to day and season to season. The anthocyanins produced on sunny days are more vivid than those produced on dull, overcast days.

After all the leaf pigments have decayed, the leaves will break off and fall to the ground.

What is the meaning of the Canadian coat of arms?

Canada has a complex coat of arms, and there is much symbolism in the design. The coat of arms was drawn up by a committee set up by the Canadian Prime Minister and the British Heraldry Office. The design was officially received from King George V in 1921.

The shield in the centre of the design shows the arms of the four countries that colonized Canada: France, England, Scotland, and Ireland. The shield is supported by the British Lion and the Scottish Unicorn.

The lion that rests on top of the helmet is wearing a crown. That lion represents the Monarch of the Dominion. The Latin motto, *A MARI USQUE AD MARE*, means "from sea to sea."

Above the lion is a maple leaf, which represents the soldiers killed in World War I.

Why does Wile E. Coyote get all his supplies from the Acme company?

Wile E. Coyote, that hungry creature who can't afford to buy a meal but can mail-order just about anything, is the creation of Chuck Jones, the animator famous for cartoon characters such as Bugs Bunny, Daffy Duck, Sylvester the cat, Elmer Fudd, Pepe Le Pew, and Porky Pig. According to Jones, Wile E.'s pursuit of the Roadrunner represents a kind of stubbornness—following a course of action long after the original reason for embarking upon it is forgotten. It is his sense of lost dignity that forces the Coyote to continue his efforts to capture the Roadrunner.

The Acme Company is Wile E.'s chief supplier of goods that never quite work right. In his autobiography, *Chuck Amuck*, Jones says that his portrayal of machinery as never functioning properly reflects his own frustration with tools.

The word "acme" comes from Greek and means "the highest point or peak." For a time, it was common for new companies to adopt the name Acme to suggest that they were the best in their field. This practice also put them at the front of their sections in the Yellow Pages. These days, businesses use names like AAABBCCDD Drugs for the same reason, although, as Jones notes, that makes them sound a bit like an establishments run by Porky Pig.

Jones credits the name Acme to his sister. She named everything Acme, in parody of the then-common business practice, when she and Jones were children. Many businesses in Jones' other cartoons for Warner Brothers were also named Acme, and the practice became a running joke. But it was in the Roadrunner cartoons, first released in 1949 and produced until 1963, that the Acme Corporation reached its acme.

The door to the Chuck Jones studio once had a sign on it that read, "Acme Corporation," followed by the slogan, "We Build Fine Acmes."

Jones is widely regarded as one of the finest animators ever in America, and he is known for his subtle comic timing and his understanding of character. He has produced cartoons featuring most of the Warner Brothers characters, and his cartoons earned him three Academy Awards.

Jones also directed and put his personal stamp on the Dr. Seuss TV specials *The Grinch Who Stole Christmas* and *Horton Hears a Who*. In association with the National Film Board of Canada, Jones also worked on the children's television program *Curiosity Shop*.

Whatever happened to the original Gerber Food baby?

Over the years, there have been many babies who starred in Gerber's television commercials. Some have even made appearances on the talk show circuit as whatever-happened-to guests with their different stories to tell.

However, the original Gerber Food baby was the baby whose picture first appeared on Gerber food products in 1928. Her name is Ann Turner-Cook, and she is now a retired school teacher living in Florida. Her baby face has graced the labels of Gerber products, unchanged, for over 60 years. Every year, the company prints another 1.8 billion copies of her picture.

Things have changed for Turner-Cook since her first appearance on grocery shelves. She has had babies of her own—in fact, even her babies have had babies. But despite the intervening years, she still looks enough like her photo that the panelists of *What's My Line* had no trouble identifying her.

How does liquid fabric softener get rid of static cling?

Static electricity is caused when two objects rub together. The resulting friction causes one to lose a few electrons to the other. As clothes go round and round in a washer, they rub together. Some lose electrons, leaving them with a positive charge. Others collect electrons, leaving them with a negative charge. The type of fabric a piece of clothing is made from will determine whether it collects or releases electrons, and therefore whether its charge is positive or negative. Most clothes will become negatively charged.

There is also static build-up in a dryer. During a 40-minute cycle, clothes tumble more than two thousand times. The warm air creates a good environment for electron exchange.

Fabric softener breaks up in water to yield positively charged molecules. These positively charged molecules are attracted to the negatively charged molecules of the cloth, cancelling out the two charges.

The fabric softener used in the wash cycle also works to reduce friction as clothes rub together. Liquid softener is very slippery. As it is dispersed in the water during the wash cycle, the softener coats the fabrics, making for less friction. Less friction means less static.

In the dryer, the softener melts into the fabric, preventing static electricity from building up after the clothes are dry.

HOW DOES LIQUID SOFTENER GET RID OF
STATIC CLING?

How do government systems in Australia and New Zealand differ from Canada's?

Both governments from down under have the same sort of parliamentary system as Canada has, but with their own special variations.

In Canada, proposed legislation is first given three readings in the House of Commons. The bill is introduced with little discussion during the first reading, there is more detailed debate during the second reading, and then the bill goes into committee. The committee, made of government members from all major parties, work out the details and logistics of implementing the legislation. Then, at the third reading, the bill is presented, with the committee's recomendations to the House, to be voted upon.

Once the bill is passed in the House of Commons, it is given three more readings in the Senate. If the bill also wins the Senate vote, it is signed by the Governor-General, who is the Queen's representative in Canada. Then the bill is law.

The process in Australia is the same as in Canada. Bills are given three readings in the House of Representatives, which is similar to our House of Commons. Then they go to the Australian Senate for three readings. The bills become law after they've been given royal assent and are signed by the Australian Governor-General. However, unlike Canadians, Australians get to elect their senators.

New Zealand has a more streamlined government. Bills are also given three readings in the Parliament, but there is no upper house. New Zealanders found their chamber of sober second thought, called the Legislative Council, to be ineffective, so they abolished it on January 1, 1951.

How many cells are there in a human body?

A newborn baby enters the world with about two trillion cells. By the time it is an adult, that body is made up of 60 trillion cells. Twenty-five trillion of those are blood cells. There are over 200 types of cells in the body.

Cells are continuously being lost through shedding and elimination. The body replaces one per cent, or 600 billion, of its cells each day.

In addition to its own cells, the body is also host to one hundred million cells of other organisms. Most of these organisms are harmless, and some even help the host body protect itself from other, harmful, organisms.

Why does Parmesan cheese last longer than other types of cheese?

Cheese, like almost any other food, can go mouldy. A cheese with a high moisture content is much more likely to go mouldy than one with a low moisture content. Parmesan cheese has a moisture content of about 32 per cent. This is low compared with the 42 to 46 per cent moisture content of mozzarella or cheddar.

As well, Parmesan has a high salt content. Salt prevents the growth of moulds. It is a preservative that gives Parmesan a shelf life of 10 to 18 months. Cheddar will go mouldy in about five weeks, while mozzarella will last only two to three weeks.

Who created the metric system?

The metric system is the decimal-based system of weights and measures. A French clergyman by the name of Gabriel Mouton introduced the first metric unit in 1670. He calculated his unit of measurement by dividing the length of the arc of one minute of longitude on the earth's surface into tenths.

Two other Frenchmen, named Delambre and Mechain, refined the system in 1791. They took the distance from the North Pole to the equator, called a meridional quadrant, as measured on the median from Barcelona to Dunkirk, and divided it into millionths to get one metre. A plan to standardize all measures was approved in 1791, and the metric system became law in France in 1799.

The system was soon adopted by other countries. However, in France, many people preferred their own regional systems of measurement. The French government responded by outlawing the use of any system other than metric, effective 1840.

Contrary to popular belief, the United States is one of the countries that accepted metric measurement early on. A law was passed in 1866 recognizing the validity of the system. Thus, all contracts that use metric are legally binding in the US. The US law did not, however, outlaw any other system.

The metric system is still evolving. The scientific community still holds conferences to determine how to metricize other measurable quantities, such as time. Even the established metric measurements are subject to revision. A metre is now defined as the distance light travels in a vacuum in 1/299,792,458 of a second.

How did the Indian summer get its name?

The name for the period of warm weather after the first frost of fall dates back to at least 1778. The Indian summer was the period when North American Indians prepared for the coming winter. The book, *Curiosities of Popular Custom*, published in 1897, says that Indians regarded the temporary return of mild weather as a gift from the god of the southwest. This is the god who sends the warm southwest winds, and who takes his people away after death.

Meteorologically speaking, an Indian summer is the result of omega blocks—two low pressure systems on the continent that anchor a high pressure system in between them. When these pressure systems are stationary, the result is warm, sunny days. But for such a condition to be officially recognized as an Indian summer, there must first be a frost. After the frost, there can be several Indian summers in one season.

Who are the kings on playing cards?

According to the world's largest manufacturer of playing cards, the US Playing Card Company, the kings on playing cards are based on real figures from history. These kings represent the Hebrew, Greek, Roman, and Holy Roman Empires.

The King of Spades is David, King of Israel. Because David played the harp, that instrument is usually included somewhere on the card. David is also shown with the sword of Goliath in his hand.

The Greek Empire is represented by Alexander the Great. His card is the King of Clubs. Since he was the first conqueror of the known world, he is found with an orb, a celestial body, somewhere on his costume.

Julius Caesar is the King of Diamonds. He is always shown in profile because it is said that the only picture of Julius was the profile that appeared on Roman coins.

Finally, the King of Hearts is Charlemagne, King of the Franks and Emperor of the Holy Roman Empire. Originally, the King of Hearts was shown swinging a battleaxe. Later, the cards showed just the axe handle. Later still, the handle was changed to a sword.

How do you determine the sex of a scorpion?

Very carefully.

A male scorpion usually has a larger abdomen than does a female. But such a method of determination requires that you have one of each sex handy. A more reliable means of telling the boys from the girls requires closer examination.

First, turn the scorpion over so you can see the bottom of its abdomen, which is called the prosoma. Look between the junction of the abdomen and the last pair of legs for plates shaped like a spade. These plates are called genital opercula, and these modified appendages cover the genital opening. If the genital operculum has little hooks on the end, you have a male scorpion on your hands, figuratively speaking. If not, you have a female.

Male scorpions have these extra appendages so they can hold on when mating with female scorpions. Which they do very carefully, of course.

What is the origin of the the word "news"?

According to the old rhyme, "news is conveyed by letter, word, or mouth, and comes to us from north, east, west, and south." Some newspapers used to have the letters arranged like a compass on their mastheads, suggesting that the news they carried came from the four corners of the world.

The compass may help us remember how to spell, but it is not the source of the word. "News" has a rather ordinary origin. The word comes from the Old English "newes," meaning novelties. The singular form, newe, is also an adjective, meaning . . . new.

How long does it take a skunk to recharge after spraying its scent?

Skunks are well-known for their foul-smelling spray. This liquid—butyl mercaptan—is produced in an organ similar to the human prostate, and is chemically related to sweat. Mercaptan is also found in asparagus.

Skunks are first able to squirt when they are four to five weeks old.

When a skunk feels threatened, it furiously stamps its front feet, bushes up its tail, and issues a fine mist from behind. Some skunk species stand on their front feet when they shoot.

The skunk can hit a target ten feet away. Once the deed is done, the skunk is good for another one or two shots, if required. If the skunk exhausts itself, it can produce enough mercaptan for another blast within an hour. It takes a skunk with an empty tank a day to fully load up.

There's good news for anyone who might nonetheless *want* to get close to a skunk. Some hunters and veterinarians report that a skunk can be safely handled if held by the tail. In this position, the animal is unable to use the muscles required to release the spray.

HOW LONG DOES IT TAKE A SKUNK TO RECHARGE
AFTER SPRAYING ITS SCENT?

Why are AM radio stations all on even numbers and FM stations all on odd numbers on the dial?

Many radio stations round off or abbreviate their numbers in their advertising and promotion. An FM station may call itself 102, but its actual position will be be 102.1 or 101.9. In the case of FM stations, the decimal is always part of the number, and this number is always odd. AM stations' numbers are always even.

The AM band dial starts at 535 and ends at 1605. Each AM station takes up ten kilohertz of radio wave space. That means a station located at the lowest point of the dial would be licensed to broadcast between 535 and 545 kilohertz, so its call number would be in the middle, 540. This is the carrier frequency, which is always in the centre of the band. Every station up the dial is located a multiple of ten kilohertz from this station.

The FM dial starts at 88.0 and goes to 108.0 megahertz, and stations are spaced a multiple of .2 megahertz apart. A station at the low end of the dial would be spaced from 88.0 to 88.2, so its carrier frequency would be 88.1 megahertz.

Where does the expression "the whole nine yards" come from?

According to etymologists, the people who study word and phrase origins, there are several ways to explain "the whole nine yards."

The first explanation comes from the garment trade. Bolts of cloth come in nine-yard lengths. A fancy dress that uses up the entire bolt of cloth takes the whole nine yards.

Another theory comes from the construction industry. A cement truck with a rotating mixer carries enough cement to cover nine square yards of foundation. A major project would therefore take up the whole nine yards of cement.

Still another possibility comes from another line of work. At one time, the standard way to construct a prison was to put a retaining wall just inside the outside wall where the "bulls"—convict jargon for guards—would stand. The space between the retaining wall and the outside wall was nine yards wide, and the retaining wall was also nine yards high. It was said that if an escaping prisoner made it over the retaining wall and across the space to the outer wall, then he had gone the whole nine yards.

Whatever happened to NASA's Project Needles?

Project West Ford was a NASA plan of the early 1960s. In brief, the idea was to create a belt of millions of small copper wires around the earth. The plan, devised by researchers at MIT, was designed to help the American military relay radio signals around the planet, even in the event of a nuclear war.

These copper wires were one fifth the width of a human hair and seven tenths of an inch long. Once the wires were in orbit around the earth, radio signals could be bounced off them and around the earth. If there were a nuclear attack and the belt were disrupted, the needles would eventually float back into place. Thus, the belt would be self-repairing, whereas a communications satellite could be permanently damaged or destroyed.

The project actually became a reality. On October 21, 1961, an Atlas Agena B-rocket released mothball material containing 480 million wires 2000 miles above the earth. As the mothball material disintegrated, a copper belt nine miles wide and 15 feet deep was formed around the earth.

Scientists knew the belt was working when they picked up some wayward signals of a TV western. But the greatest threat to Project West Ford lay on the ground. The project became more widely known by the nickname given to it by the MIT engineers—Project Needles. This proved to be a major P.R. faux pas. The popular perception was that it was no longer safe to walk outside without an umbrella. Astronomers, who should have known better, complained that they would not be able to see the stars. The Soviet Union expressed concern that its cosmonauts would be riddled by the needles. There was much public controversy, newspaper columns were written, and cartoons even appeared in The *New Yorker*. The fact that the tiny copper wires were a quarter of a mile apart did little to settle fears.

The general resistance to the project, plus the glamorous success of the newly-launched Telstar communications satellite, spelled the doom of Project Needles. The experiment had been designed so that the orbit of the copper wires would decay, and they would re-enter the atmosphere in a few years. In 1966, controversy flared up again as people feared they would be bombarded by millions of pointy, burning metal pins. In fact, the wires were too small and light to burn in the atmosphere, and they did reach the earth. According to calculations, they fell about five miles apart at their most dense, which was around the North and South Poles. Not a single copper wire has ever been recovered.

What were Canada geese called before Confederation?

Well, one thing's for sure—they weren't called British North America geese. Their name, Canada geese, was bestowed upon them long before the founding of the country, although both names share the same origins.

In 1758, the geese were given their English name, which was based on what the Indians called the birds. "Kanata" is a Huron word that means "village" or "settlement." The Hurons named the geese Kanata because the birds bred near Indian settlements.

Kanata was also the name the Indians gave to the French settlement of Stadacona, now known as Quebec City. In both cases, "Kanata" was corrupted to "Canada." Given the sequence of events, it looks like the country was named after the bird rather than vice versa.

Why are coin banks in the shape of pigs?

The pig's role as a child's first savings account is a visual pun, even though the animal is known more for being muddy than thrifty.

A dense orange clay called pygg was once used extensively in Europe for pottery. The clay was cheap, abundant, and useful for such household goods as dishes and jars. The earthenware made from this clay also came to be known as pygg.

Before the days of banking for common folk, spare cash was hidden in pygg jars. By the 18th century, the jars in which money was stored were made of a number of substances, but the jars continued to be called pygg jars, often spelled p-i-g. Potters with an eye for a pun made pig jars by casting them in the form of pigs.

BEEFY BANK

Why are traffic lights red and green?

Coloured lights were first used to control traffic in the early 1800s. These lights were lanterns with red and green glass lenses, and they were found along railway lines.

The first traffic lights for road traffic were set up near the British Parliament Buildings at George and Bridge Streets in London in 1868.

Red and green were chosen because of the emotional responses associated with them. Red is the colour of danger because of its association with blood—you usually see blood only in dangerous situations. Red was also a warning sign in feudal Germany. A red circle with a slash through it was placed on fences to mark boundaries and warn intruders to stay clear. This mark was the forerunner of the modern stop sign.

Green is a more soothing colour, suggesting safety, possibly because of its association with nature. Green is also at the opposite end of the colour spectrum from red, making it easy to distinguish the two colours when visibility is poor.

What is the purpose of the kitchen witch?

The kitchen witch is a good luck charm that looks like a witch on a broom. Instead of wearing the black robes and hat of a Halloween witch, however, the kitchen witch wears a bright apron and a head scarf or babushka.

The custom of hanging a witch in the kitchen has been practised in Scandinavia for centuries. The witch ensures success in the kitchen—cakes won't fall, gravy won't be lumpy, eggs won't stick to the pan, and so on.

The reasoning behind the kitchen witch was simple—one witch will not encroach on territory already claimed by another witch. A fake homemade figure of a witch will fool the real thing every time.

Kitchen witches are still used for decoration and are widely available at stores specializing in kitchen goods.

What is the origin of the barbecue?

The word "barbecue" comes from the language of the extinct native tribe of Haiti, the Taino. In the mid-17th century, Spanish pirates discovered the Taino practice of smoking an animal whole on a spit supported by a frame of sticks called a barbacoa.

French explorers also found the same cooking method in Guiana, and spelled the word "babracot." The modern English word is a French pun, based on the manner in which an animal is mounted on the spit: barbe a queue, beard to tail.

What is the origin of the Christmas candy cane?

Sugar candy was once given to children by their parents to keep the fidgety youngsters quiet during long services at church. This was long before anyone realized that the sugar dose in the candy would only make the problem worse.

During the 17th century, a choirmaster in Cologne, Germany had an idea to combine the candy with some Christmas lessons. He had some stick candy shaped into the form of a shepherd's crook to remind children of the birth in Bethlehem.

It was also the custom in Germany at the time to decorate Christmas trees with food. The practice is not as widespread now as it once was, but because of its ideal shape, the tradition continues with candy canes.

Candy canes were originally white; the red stripes were introduced in the early 20th century. While the colour may be different, the recipe for candy canes has hardly changed over the years. The candy is made almost entirely of sugar and corn syrup, with a dash of peppermint oil for flavour and a touch of red dye for the striping.

How are mandarin oranges peeled and canned without getting crushed?

When considering the contents of a can of First Choice mandarin oranges, you may think the peeling and canning process is flawless. But it isn't. Some pieces *are* broken and crushed.

The entire process of canning oranges is mechanized. The first step is blanching. The oranges are dipped in vats of simmering water, then quickly put in cold water. This breaks down the membrane holding the peel to the flesh of the fruit, which makes peeling easier. Pears, peaches, and other fruits are also blanched in this manner.

The oranges are then peeled and the sections are pulled apart. The transparent membrane that surrounds each section is then chemically removed. Finally, the whole sections are canned in syrup and sent to market.

Broken sections are also canned as orange pieces, used for juice, or make their way into the cans of mandarin sections as syrup. Sections that survive the entire process in one piece are marketed as First Choice. They are usually more expensive than broken sections, which are second or third choice, depending on their condition.

How many people have there ever been?

According to the Population Reference Bureau in Washington, DC, the total number of people ever born is around 100 billion. With the world's population at over five billion today, that means about five per cent of the people who have ever walked this earth are still treading on it.

The Bureau uses 200,000 BC as the beginning of humankind for its calculations. That is based on the belief that the first primates that can be considered homo sapiens appeared at about that time.

The population of the world at the time of Christ was about 200 million. By 1650, it had risen to 500 million. Two centuries later, it was a billion. By 1930, it had doubled again to two billion. It took only 45 years for the population to double again to four billion.

The world is now home to 5.3 billion people. If the population continues to grow at its present rate, we will add another billion people to the total by the end of this century.

Do ostriches really hide their heads in the sand?

The image of a gawky bird that thinks it is safe from the world if its head is buried makes for good cartoons, but it's an inaccurate picture.

The ostrich is a difficult animal to study because it is so wary, but it seems an ostrich *will* attempt to hide in tall grass or behind a large object if it is threatened. The ostrich also lowers its head when hiding, seemingly not realizing that its body may still be exposed to an enemy.

An ostrich will also poke its head into holes in the ground, but only in search of food, not to hide. The emu, another large bird similar to the ostrich, lays its head flat on the ground when sleeping.

The head-in-the-sand image makes the ostrich look cowardly, but the bird is actually very aggressive. The ostrich will kick, bite, and scratch when angry. If that doesn't deter an enemy, the ostrich will puff out its chest and attempt to crush the foe by pinning it against a rock or tree.

DO OSTRICHES REALLY HIDE THEIR HEADS
IN THE SAND?

Who invented Velcro?

The idea for Velcro, those interlocking strips of tiny eyes and hooks, came to George de Mestral, a Swiss mountaineer, as he picked burrs from his socks. De Mestral noticed that the burrs were covered with tiny hooks that attached themselves to the fabric of his socks and to the fur of his dog.

De Mestral realized he had the fastening solution that would make buttons, hooks, and zippers obsolete. Unfortunately, the technology was not available in 1948 to produce hooks and eyes small enough yet strong enough for repeated use on a scale that was economically feasible. It took a decade and improvements in nylon to make de Mestral's fastener a reality.

The name Velcro comes from the words "velvet" and "crochet," the French word for hook.

The position of zippers and buttons in the textile industry is secure, but Velcro has found applications in places where quick and easy fastening and unfastening is required. It has even been used in the space program to hold astronauts in place as they work in weightlessness. Regular Velcro is made of nylon, but Velcro can be made of other substances. For example, the Velcro used to insulate radioactive piping at nuclear power stations is made of stainless steel and silver.

Did Dr. Hook ever make it to the cover of *Rolling Stone*?

Dr. Hook is the rock band that hit the record charts with the song *The Cover of the Rolling Stone*, in 1972. Although some of the group's later music was relatively mainstream, its early work parodied the cliches of rock and roll. Dr. Hook released its first album in 1972, and the first hit single was a whiney ballad of lost love called *Sylvia's Mother*. All the songs on the album were written by Shel Silverstein, a cartoonist and writer whose work ranges from satire in *Playboy* to a series of children's books.

Silverstein's most successful musical work includes *The Unicorn, A Boy Named Sue, The Ballad of Lucy Jordan*, and *Queen of the Silver Dollar*, recorded by the Irish Rovers, Johnny Cash, Marianne Faithful, and Emmylou Harris respectively. Among the other stars who have recorded Silverstein's songs are Brenda Lee, Peter, Paul, & Mary, Waylon Jennings, Loretta Lynn, and Hank Snow.

Dr. Hook's second hit, also from the first album, was *The Cover of the Rolling Stone*. The song, satirizing the excesses of rock culture, was about a band that was doing all the right rock star things. They kept "getting richer, but we can't get our picture on the cover of the *Rolling Stone*."

An appearance on the cover of *Rolling Stone* magazine, rock's too-serious journal of news and criticism, is considered proof that a band or musician has made it to the top, not only in financial terms, but artistically as well. Dr. Hook was the cover story of the March 29th, 1973 issue of *Rolling Stone* magazine.

What is a blue moon, and how often does one happen?

In the past, depending on atmospheric conditions, the moon could appear to be white, yellow, orange, or red, but never blue. "When the moon is blue" originally meant never, or when you-know-where freezes over.

However, it was eventually discovered that ash from certain volcanic eruptions could make the moon appear to be blue. That discovery led to the expression "once in a blue moon," which means almost never, or at least not very often.

Blue moon is also the name given to a second full moon that occurs within one calendar month. That happens every 30 to 32 months, or once in a blue moon.

Why is January 1st the beginning of the year?

The Romans were the first to begin the new year on January 1st. They chose that date in 153 BC because it was the day that the city's consuls began their one-year appointments to govern the city. Prior to that, the year began on March 1st. September, October, November, and December were then the seventh, eighth, ninth, and tenth months of the year, as their names suggest.

Until 1752, the first day of the new year in Britain was March 25th. That meant, for example, the day after March 24, 1750 was March 25, 1751. The first day of the year was changed to January 1st in 1752, when Britain and all her colonies adopted the Gregorian Calendar, the calendar we use today.

Why do smells evoke strong emotional memories?

Stimulation of any of our senses can take us back for a moment to the past. These recollections can be pleasant, as when a favourite song is playing on the radio, or they can be frightening, such as when you hear a noise that reminds you of a dentist's drill.

Smell has long been recognized as the sense that brings back the most emotional memories. The smell of a bakery brings back memories of grandma's kitchen. Even smells that by themselves would be considered unappealing, such as those of a barn, can bring back fond memories of days gone by. This is because of the way olfactory nerves are connected to the brain.

The nerve pathways responsible for transmitting olfactory stimuli to the brain all begin in the nose and mouth. The main olfactory nerve sends its information to the part of the brain called the main olfactory bulb. The accessory olfactory nerve leads from the nose to a small part of the olfactory bulb called the accessory olfactory bulb. The information carried to the olfactory bulbs continues directly to a part of the brain called the hypothalamus.

In evolutionary terms, the hypothalamus is the oldest part of the brain. It is found in all animals from fish to mammals. The hypothalamus regulates many basic functions and controls motivation in matters of survival. The hypothalamus is thus responsible for things like hunger, aggression, and sex drive. Because the hypothalamus also regulates emotional responses, emotions and smells become closely associated.

Why do cats come up to people who don't like cats, and stay away from people who do?

According to some feline experts, cats are very good at reading the body language of strangers but are weak on interpretation.

The person who is uncomfortable with cats may shy away from or ignore the animal in the hopes that it will go away. The cat will notice this behaviour and understand it to mean that this person is not a threat and can therefore be approached for affection.

The person who reaches out to the cat and tries to be friendly will arouse the cat's suspicion. This person will be perceived as an invader who must be avoided. The person who persists in encroaching on the cat's territory only bears out the cat's suspicion, and will continue to be avoided.

WHY DO CATS COME UP TO PEOPLE WHO DON'T LIKE CATS, AND STAY AWAY FROM PEOPLE WHO DO?

Why is lead used in crystal?

Lead is used in the manufacture of fine crystal for reasons of practicality and aesthetics.

Lead makes crystal more durable than regular glass. Ordinary glass is so brittle that it breaks very easily along any line that might have been scratched into it. In fact, this is how glass is normally cut. If glass were hand-cut like crystal, it would shatter before the job was finished. Lead acts as an adhesive when added to molten glass, holding the glass molecules together. This characteristic makes the crystal more flexible and manageable. Crystal gives off a "ping" when tapped because it is more flexible and vibrates more than glass.

Crystal also owes its lustre and brilliance to lead. Manufacturers cut crystal to show this characteristic to its best advantage. This would not be possible without the adhesive quality of lead.

Why do mints feel cool as they dissolve in the mouth?

The sugars in candy require heat as well as moisture to dissolve in your mouth. This heat is taken from the tissues that are in contact with the candy as it dissolves in your saliva.

However, only some candies, such as mints, feel noticeably cooler as they dissolve. There are some compounds in mints, such as menthol, that activate receptors in the oral and nasal cavities. When these receptors are activated, a message is sent to the brain claiming that the temperature in the nose and mouth has dropped. This is also why menthol is added to cigarettes—it makes the smoke feel cooler to the throat.

How do we get our second wind?

Our second wind, or the reserve of energy that kicks in after a period of exertion, is believed to come from three sources, only two of which actually represent sources of energy.

The first source of energy is glycogen. Glycogen is a polysaccharide stored in the muscles. When muscles become fatigued, the body begins to convert glycogen into glucose. The glucose provides a second source of energy to the body as it begins to tire.

Second, as the body uses energy, carbon dioxide and lactic acid gather in the blood vessels of the muscles. This accumulation signals the body to allow more oxygen into these vessels so the muscles can work harder. Oxygen is an important ingredient as cells convert carbohydrates into energy. As more oxygen reaches the cells, the body starts to operate more efficiently with less fatigue.

The third part of the second wind comes from natural pain-killers called endorphins. Pain will normally inhibit effort, but the body produces endorphins to reduce pain and create a sense of well-being. Endorphins are produced in the brain and work in a similar manner to morphine. These endorphins are the source of the so-called natural high experienced by endurance athletes such as long-distance runners.

How does the Richter scale work?

The Richter scale provides a simple means of describing the magnitude of an earthquake. The scale was developed in 1935 by Charles Richter, a seismologist at the California Institute of Technology.

Richter arbitrarily chose an earthquake that had recently occurred to serve as the standard against which other earthquakes would be measured. That earthquake was assigned a measurement of 3.0 on his scale. Richter designed his scale to be logarithmic— that means each increase of one unit means the earthquake is ten times as strong. Therefore, an earthquake ten times as strong as the reference earthquake would be given a measurement of 4.0 on the Richter scale. An earthquake that measures 5.0 on the scale would be ten times the magnitude of an earthquake that measured 4.0 on the scale. And so on.

Measurement of an earthquake's magnitude is based on vertical ground motion, as measured on a seismograph 100 kilometres from the epicentre, or source point, of the quake. Although the ground moves in all directions during a quake, only the vertical motion is considered in this calculation.

An earthquake that measures 3.0 on the Richter scale will produce vertical ground motion of less than a centimetre. An earthquake that measures 5.0 on the Richter scale will produce vertical motion of about eight centimetres. An earthquake that measures 8.0 on the Richter scale is of major proportions; its vertical ground motion is measured in metres.

The strongest earthquake recorded since the Richter scale was introduced occurred in Assam, India, on August 15, 1950. Over 1500 people died in the quake, which measured 8.7 on the Richter scale. The strongest earthquake for which there is a seismographic record that can be measured occurred in Japan on March 2, 1933. That quake measured 8.9 on the Richter scale and killed 2,990 people.

The most devastating earthquake in history

occurred in Shaanxi, China, on January 24, 1556. There is not enough seismographic evidence to measure this quake on the Richter scale, but 830,000 people are believed to have died.

Who invented ice skates?

Skates were in use as far back as 1000 BC in Scandinavia. Early Finns and Laplanders developed this technique for gliding over snow and ice. Blades were made from the rib and shank bones of animals such as elk, oxen, and reindeer. Skiing is also derived from this form of travel.

Skating on the canals of the Netherlands dates back to the middle ages. Donning a pair of skates was a practical means of getting about to do one's business when the canals froze over and all other roadways were slick with ice. Recreational skating spread throughout northwestern Europe by the 17th century. Skating was a popular pastime enjoyed by the courtiers of Marie Antoinette and Napoleon Bonaparte.

Skate blades have been made of many materials, from wood to various metals. The first all-iron skate blade, which strapped onto the bottom of an ordinary boot, was introduced in Philadelphia in 1848.

When did oral hygiene begin?

The modern medicine cabinet is cluttered with mouthwashes, dental floss, toothpaste, toothbrushes, and water-picks. Most of this stuff is recent, but some form of preventative dental care has been available since ancient times.

For brushing teeth and gums, Egyptians used twigs frayed at the ends. The practice, which started around 3000 BC, continues today in some African cultures.

The first bristle toothbrush was introduced in China in 1498. The bristles were made from hog hairs. From China, the bristle toothbrush spread to Europe. The Europeans preferred softer horsehair bristles. The first patent for a toothbrush was issued in 1857. The nylon toothbrush was first sold in 1938, and the electric toothbrush hit the market in 1961.

Egyptians also had the first toothpaste, made of powdered pumice and vinegar. From Roman times to the 18th century, human urine was a key ingredient in toothpaste, and was also used as a mouthwash. Fortunately, today we have Listerine.

Modern toothpaste has been marketed since the late 1800s. The early formulations included silica or quartz for their abrasive qualities. Fluoride was added to many brands of toothpaste in the 1960s.

WHEN DID ORAL HYGIENE BEGIN?

Who invented the microwave oven?

Percy Spencer is the father of the microwave oven. Spencer had only a grade school education, but by the time he died in 1970, there were a hundred patents in his name.

In 1946, Spencer was visiting a magnetron testing lab in Britain. The magnetron was developed by J.T. Randall in 1940 as part of Britain's radar defences during the war. The magnetron consisted of a magnet in a vacuum tube, and was used to generate high frequency radiation, like that used for radar. Spencer went to see the magnetron in action during his visit. The magnetron tube was switched on, experiments were conducted, and the chocolate bar in Spencer's pocket melted.

Curious rather than irritated, Spencer returned the next day with a bag of popping corn. The magnetron popped the corn. Like a true scientist, Spencer returned the next day to repeat the experiment, this time with a dozen eggs. The experiment was a success, with one egg blowing up in the face of an engineer who got too close. Spencer realized that the egg exploded because it had cooked rapidly from the inside out.

Spencer, who was working for Raytheon Incorporated of Lexington, Massachusetts, returned to the United States and developed a working microwave oven called the Radar Range. The device, driven by vacuum tubes, was the size of a refrigerator, with a cooking space the size of the freezer portion. The Radar Range was sold mainly to restaurants.

Microwave ovens for domestic use were introduced in 1967. The Radar Range name continued to be used as Raytheon merged with the Amana appliance company, producing the Amana Radar Range.

Why are ice cubes used in restaurants and bars not fogged in the centre?

Ice cubes from the home freezer are often fogged or cloudy because the water they are made from has not been properly prepared. Water from the kitchen tap contains tiny air bubbles. The cloudiness in the centre of the ice cube is caused by these air bubbles, which are trapped in the water as it freezes.

Cold water will hold air in solution for a longer period than will hot water. Air bubbles in hot water escape more easily because the heat causes them to expand and rise to the surface. Consequently, filling an ice cube tray with hot water will produce a clearer ice cube. Furthermore, if water, hot or cold, is allowed to stand for a long enough period, eventually all the air bubbles will escape from the water. The clearest home-made ice cube comes from water that has been allowed to sit for a day or so.

But restaurants, bars, and other businesses cannot take the time to produce the perfect cube themselves. They purchase ice that has been commercially prepared by ice-making companies. These companies pour water into tanks to prepare it for freezing. Inside the tanks are copper pipes, through which an electric current is run. The current draws the air bubbles to the copper pipe, leaving the water virtually bubble-free. The water is then frozen, and the resulting clear ice is chopped, packaged, and sent to market.

Why do the spines of English books read from top to bottom, whereas the spines of French books read from bottom to top?

The French tradition of printing a book's title on its spine so that it reads from the bottom of the book to the top serves two purposes. First, in medieval times, books on bookshelves were stored stacked on top of each other face down rather than standing up. Spines were written from bottom to top so that they could be read on the bookshelf.

Second, the French style of writing a spine allows a book lying on a table to be easily identified, no matter how it sits. If the book is face up, the cover can be read. If the book is face down, the spine can be read.

The British style, with the spine reading from top to bottom, began when books were made sturdy enough to be stored standing on edge, as they are today. To read a series of titles on a shelf, one's head is tilted to the right, in the direction of the books. To scan the titles of books bound the French way, the reader's head would have to be tilted to the left, which many people find less natural.

What happens to the leftover space when oil and natural gas are extracted from the ground?

Oil and gas are not found in underground lakes, so there are no holes or caves left behind when pumping is completed.

The oil and gas are found saturated throughout small pores in underground rocks. The pores in these underground rocks are about half a millimetre or smaller in diameter. With our current technology, it is not possible to completely suck these pores dry.

Oil and gas in deep underground fields are under a great deal of pressure. When some of the oil and gas is removed, the pressure of the field decreases. The oil or gas that remains then expands to fill the space in the rock pores that have been emptied.

When there is no longer sufficient pressure to force oil and gas through the well and up to the surface, the well is said to be "dry." That, however, is just a figure of speech that reflects the limitations of the technology, not of the resource.

Why is $ the symbol for the dollar?

There are several theories to explain the origin of the dollar sign, but the most prevalent gives it a Spanish background. The peso was once the common form of currency in America. It was also known as the Spanish-American dollar. The abbreviation for pesos was PS, which was further shortened to an S with a bar through it. The S with two bars through it was a later elaboration.

Why do TV shows have canned laughter?

The laugh track that tells you that a sitcom actor's line is supposed to be funny has been the subject of ridicule for many years. Among observers of the broadcasting industry, there are those who feel the use of canned laughter is also a question of ethics.

The use of prompted audience response began even before TV, in the theatres of Paris around 1820. These theatres used to hire people to applaud, laugh, and cry at the appropriate time, so that the production seemed more successful to the paying audience than it really was. These hired applauders were called a claque.

However, it would be unfair to say that canned laughter is just another form of claque. In the early days of radio, most programs were broadcast without a studio audience. The comedies in particular sounded hollow without audience response so producers introduced the studio audience to bring the spontaneity of vaudeville and theatre to radio.

· When radio variety programs such as *The Jack Benny Show* moved to television, they brought their studio audiences with them. Originally, producers did not try this with radio sitcoms becasue they felt it would be too complicated to film those kinds of TV shows in front of a live audience.

I Love Lucy overcame this problem. Unlike other filmed programs, which are shot scene by scene over and over like a movie, *I Love Lucy* was filmed live with three cameras. The three films were then edited together and included the laughter of the studio audience.

Amos and Andy was one of the first programs to add a laugh track after the program was filmed and edited. But this laugh track was real. Each episode was shown in a theatre and the audience response was recorded. The laughter was then added to the film soundtrack for the program's broadcast.

While the purpose of the studio audience was to recreate the theatre experience, producers learned they could manipulate the television audience's perception of a program by "sweetening" the laugh track. Program engineers sweeten a laugh track by adding pre-recorded responses to give a punch line or pratfall more impact. What started out as adding a chuckle here and a guffaw there developed into the art of completely fabricating a program's laugh track. Even cartoon shows such as *The Flintstones* were given a laugh track. This practice reached its peak (and its greatest public opposition) in the 1960s.

Since then, the claim at the end of a TV program that it is "recorded before a live studio audience" has been worn as a badge of honesty by the program's producers. Even these programs, however, are edited, their flubbed scenes are reshot, and their laugh tracks are sweetened.

Some TV critics and producers have claimed that a number of innovative new programs that have failed in recent years, such as *Slap Maxwell* and *The Life and Times of Molly Dodd*, did so because they had no laugh track.

When did the sport of pitching horseshoes start?

Horseshoe pitching probably derived from the game of quoits. This game was played by Roman officers during the occupation of Britain, between the first and fifth centuries AD.

Quoits is a game in which players toss rings called quoits at a stake called the hob. The rings are made of iron and weigh about three pounds. The English peasants adopted and adapted the game. Since they didn't have quoits, they used horseshoes instead.

Horseshoe pitching became popular with Americans during the Revolutionary War. Soldiers could pass time pitching horseshoes because the equipment required was already among the troops' supplies.

Today, there is even a National Horseshoe Pitchers' Association in the US, as well as both US and World Championships. The World Championships is a two-week event, with over a thousand pitchers. Canada fields about 50 entries in this match.

WHEN DID THE SPORT OF PITCHING
HORSESHOES START?

Why were Germans called Huns during the World Wars?

The original Huns were nomadic people from Asia. Led by Attila in the fourth century AD, the Huns invaded much of central Europe, including parts of the Roman Empire. The Huns were notorious for the death and destruction they inflicted upon their victims. In times of modern war, "Hun" was a fitting epithet to give an enemy thought to be without conscience.

Derogatory labels given to groups of people are usually dreamed up by other groups of people. However, the use of "Hun" to refer to Germans came from Kaiser Wilhelm II himself. Germany sent an expeditionary force to China in 1900 to help suppress the Boxer Uprising. In a speech to the troops, the Kaiser said, "No mercy must be shown. No prisoners must be taken. As the Huns under King Attila made a name for themselves which is still mighty in tradition and legend today, may the name of German be so fixed in China by your deeds, that no Chinese shall ever again dare to look a German askance."

Rudyard Kipling is believed to the the first English writer to refer to Germany as "the Hun." A poem of his, published in the London *Times* in 1902, cautioned against British involvement in German adventurism. The last stanza reads:

In sight of peace—from the Narrow Seas
O'er half the world to run—
With a cheated crew, to league anew
With the Goth and the shameless Hun!

Newspapers and politicians popularized the term "Hun" as acts of barbarism perpetrated by the German army were reported by Allied propaganda during the First World War. The word fell into disuse shortly after the end of the war, but was brought back during the Second World War.

Why did Samuel Clemens use the pen name Mark Twain?

Samuel Clemens was not the first person to write under the name of Mark Twain. A riverboat captain named Isaiah Sellers wrote items for a New Orleans newspaper under the byline of Mark Twain. He wrote of his adventures along the Mississippi in an amusingly blustery style.

In the jargon of the riverboat crew, mark twain means the river is two fathoms, or twelve feet, deep. Samuel Clemens, then a young man working on the riverboats, wrote a parody of Isaiah Sellers' articles. The parody, which was published in a rival newspaper, was signed Sergeant Fathom. As a result of Clemens' parody, Sellers never wrote another article.

Later, when he was working for a newspaper in Virginia City, Clemens was considering using a pen name. When he had heard that Isaiah Sellers had died, Clemens adopted the captain's pen name, Mark Twain.

Clemens' first piece of writing published under the new pen name was a letter to the Virginia City *Enterprise* from Carson City, datelined February 2, 1863.

Who is the Jack of Jack O'Lantern?

Jack is a figure from Irish legend. He was quite a scoundrel, known for being both a miser and a drunkard.

According to the story, Jack once tricked the Devil into climbing a tree. Jack then quickly carved a cross into the trunk of the tree. The cross kept the Devil trapped in the tree until he promised he would never again tempt Jack to sin.

Satisfied, Jack removed the cross and let the devil go. However, after his death, Jack found himself barred from Heaven because of all his previous sinning. The Devil never forgot Jack's trick, and so he also barred Jack from ever entering Hell, which, if nothing else, is at least a warm place to spend all eternity.

Trapped between Heaven and Hell, Jack was doomed to wander the earth. One cold dark night, Jack begged the Devil for a few embers. The Devil gave Jack a single lump of burning coal. Jack kept the coal in a hollowed turnip, which he used as a lantern to light the way.

The turnip turned into a pumpkin in later versions of the story.

How are marbles made, and what's in a cat's eye marble?

Marbles, originally made from stones and bones, are a children's toy that dates back to Egyptian times and seems to have been a part of every culture. The oldest marbles ever found were in a child's grave dating from 3000 BC. Greek marbles were made of jade and agate. It is from the Greek word for the white stone agate, *marmaros*, that marbles get their name. Glass marbles were first manufactured in ancient Rome. Caesar Augustus was known to have joined street children in games of marbles.

Modern marbles begin as three tons of molten glass in a tank heated to 2000 degrees Fahrenheit. The molten glass flows out of a hole in a corner of the tank and begins to solidify immediately. The size of the hole affects the size of the resulting glass bar; the most common size is one half inch in diameter.

The soft cylindrical glass bars are then chopped into pellets and rolled through a pipe to give the pieces their spherical shape. They are then allowed to cool.

Cat's eyes, the marbles with swirls of colour in their centres, are made in much the same manner. In their case, however, a second tube containing coloured glass merges with the main tube, allowing streaks of coloured glass into the clear glass. The centre takes its whorled shape as the pellets are rolled into balls.

Most marbles are made in Korea, Taiwan, or Mexico. Vitro Agate is North America's most prolific marble maker, with an output of one million marbles a day. The company has a staff of two.

Why are cashew nuts never sold in the shell?

The cashew tree is a tropical evergreen native to North America, although it is now grown in India and equatorial Africa as a cash crop. The cashew nut comes from a fruit shaped like a pear, from which it gets the name cashew pear. The nut is on the bottom, giving the fruit an overall appearance of a bell, with the nut as the clapper.

The fruit, which is used in fermented drinks, has a flavour similar to that of an apple, so it is also known as a cashew apple.

The cashew nut is encased in a three-layered shell. The middle layer contains cardol, a caustic oil that produces a rash similar to that of poison ivy. Consequently, cashews must be removed from their shells by roasting before they can be sent to market.

Other commercial products come from the cashew plant. Cashew oil is pressed from the nuts, and medicinal products are made from cashew tree bark. In India, cardol is spread on floors to protect against termites.

Do sharks sleep?

Sharks do have periods of rest, but they don't sleep in the same manner as land animals. While resting, the shark's metabolism slows down, but not to the point where the shark is no longer moving.

Usually, sharks must be constantly on the move in order to keep breathing. This movement pushes water through the shark's gills, which collect oxygen from the water. If the sharks stopped moving, they wouldn't get any oxygen and would eventually die.

Sharks have been found almost motionless in some tropical areas, however. They appear to be resting passively on the ocean floor. These sharks are in water that has a high oxygen content. In this oxygen-enriched water, the sharks do not need to be moving to receive enough oxygen, so they stop swimming and sink.

And those,

Scott Benjamin, Jason Fleury, Allan Enden, Marie Olmstead, Jim Matlock, Brent Belford, Norm Gish, Jim MacKillican, Doreen Wood, Roy Borley, Mike Kundar, Martin Rice, Elma Scarlett, Edmund Jones, Nathan Ludwig, Rita Gernandt, Gord Hayes, Rick Patterson, Debra Desautel, Gail Blake, Rick Young, Shannon Polasek, Paul Corey, David Forbes, Stephen Murgatroyd, Darren Nixon, Richard Strombeck, Marjorie Stoutinger, Ray Barabash, Keith Seewright, Teresa McKernan, Sam Burke, Brian Turnbull, Tom Thomson, Jeannie Sutton, Clyde Blackburn, Angelica Reed, Kirsten, Art Noble, Jeremy Parkin, Bob McLarity, Jeannie Wong, Lord Beaverbrook High School, Pat McKeeber, Ken Bebe, Andrea Main, Charles Guenette, Lorne Bachiu, Carl Allcock, Emily Harris, Lorne Livitt, Jeannette Page, Rick McAllan, John McCallum, Chris Georgousis, Rita Storch, Brian Quirt, Michael Isen, Bob Diotte, John Leduc, Lynn Young, James Knox, Tristan Wood, Don Goltz, Bob Smith, Laurie Draper, Bob Eton, Reg Harbeck, Linda Smith, Vince Martin, Jessica Martin, Debra Marjulis, Lois Stevenson, Ray Smith, Simon White, Marjorie McDonald, Loesje Vanderlinden, Bill Smith, Cam MacAnnel, Ed Johnson, Margaret Stoneberg, Sarah Kirkley, Tommy Patterson, Jerry McLean, Ciel Clark, Kees Vanhemert, Karen Wolfe, Don Graham, Joe Dykens, Todd Carson, Nicholas Kelly, Dave Carroll, Erica McKay, Faye MacFee, Elfrieda Crosland, and Leroy Bidlo,

are the answers to your Good Questions!

If you liked this book, you may want to order the original

That's a Good Question!

How did the TV show "The Fifth Estate" get its name? And what are the other four estates?

What is the oily film on apples from the supermarket?

Why do Bic pens have a hole in the side while other pens don't?

Why are Nova Scotians called "bluenosers"?

Why do men's and women's clothing button on different sides?

Why do most clocks with Roman numerals on the face show the number four as IIII instead of the standard IV?

Are dolphins working for the US Navy?

What were the results of the artificial iceberg experiments of World War II?

What is the origin of the word "ketchup"?

Why is the popcorn at the movies fluffier than home-popped popcorn?

Why are the keys on a typewriter arranged the way they are?

Copies of **That's a Good Question!** are available from the publisher. To order, please complete the order form on the back page.

That's a Good Question, Canada!

Where does the blood come from for operations by veterinarians?

What is the origin of the 1960s civil rights theme song *We Shall Overcome*?

How much paper can be obtained from the average-sized tree?

How do seedless fruit trees reproduce?

Who invented popcorn?

How does a spider get its first line across?

Why is there no channel one on TV sets?

What makes the rattle in a rattlesnake's tail?

Why do they make screws with different kinds of heads?

Who is the Murphy of Murphy's law?

Why do birds face the same direction when perched on a high-tension wire?

Copies of **That's a Good Question, Canada!** are available from the publisher. To order, please complete the order form on the following page.

Please print clearly; this will be your mailing label.

Name _____

Address _____

_____

_____

I'd like

_____ copies of the original That's a Good Question!
ISBN 0-9694287-0-7

_____ copies of That's a Good Question, Canada!
ISBN 0-9694287-2-3

_____ copies of What the Heck Is a Grape Nut?
ISBN 0-9694287-6-6

For _____ total copies at $11.00 each, I enclose

$_____ (Price includes postage, handling, and GST).

Once completed, mail this form to

Script: the writers' group inc.
Suite 200, 839 5th Avenue S.W.
Calgary, Alberta, Canada
T2P 3C8

Please allow two to three weeks for delivery